Essential
San
Francisco

by
CAROLE CHESTER

PASSPORT BOOKS
a division of *NTC Publishing Group*
Lincolnwood, Illinois USA

Published by Passport Books, a division of NTC Publishing Group, 4255 West
Touhy Avenue, Lincolnwood (Chicago), Illinois 60646–1975 U.S.A.

Published by Passport Books in conjunction with The Automobile Association of
Great Britain.

Written by Carole Chester
"Peace and Quiet" section by Paul Sterry

Library of Congress Catalog
Card Number 93–85599
ISBN 0–8442–8931–0

10 9 8 7 6 5 4 3 2 1

PRINTED IN TRENTO, ITALY

Front cover picture: Golden Gate Bridge

This book employs a simple
rating system to help choose
which places to visit:

◆◆◆ do not miss

◆◆   see if you can

◆   worth seeing if
     you have time

INTRODUCTION

The characteristic skyline of downtown San Francisco seen across the Bay

INTRODUCTION

San Francisco is full of actors and models and people with innovative, outlandish ideas: artists and dreamers with their heads in the fluffy clouds that puff over San Francisco Bay. The city has had little need to invite them in – they naturally gravitate there. When the West was new and brash it was in this city that the arts and culture flourished. At the end of the 19th century San Francisco could boast the US's finest opera and a symphony orchestra so popular that it was among the first in the country to receive assistance from public funds. Being such a center for the arts has given San Francisco a certain sophistication and snob appeal that other Californian metropolises have never enjoyed. It is dressier than San Diego, more polished than Los Angeles, far more highbrow than Las Vegas in neighboring Nevada. Even so, it was founded in a boisterous, raucous pioneer era when fortunes could be made – and lost.

Gold was the name of the game. The rush to California to find the irresistible yellow metal transformed San Francisco from what was little more than a mining camp into a boom town.

With gold and the need for transportation to carry it came the Wells Fargo transportation company. Eventually, the luckier fortune-hunters required places to keep their gold and banking became big business in San Francisco. The gold still glows in the color of the Bay resort beaches and the blondes who sunbathe there. California is the Golden State, and gold is celebrated in the famous Golden Gate Bridge and Park (though visitors may be disappointed to find the bridge in reality rust colored).

San Francisco's multiethnic population, which gave – and still gives – the city its special color, was the result not just of the gold rush, although the fortune-seekers came from far afield, some to settle. It was the railroad which demanded workers, immigrants from as far away as China. If any visitor had never heard of the "Big Four" before, once in San Francisco, he or she cannot escape these four railroad barons' names: Stanford, Huntingdon, Crocker and Hopkins. After building the Central Pacific they turned their attention to the Bay region. The Chinese who labored on the new railway made themselves such a niche here out West that today there are more of them than in any other Far Eastern community outside Asia, and San Francisco's Chinatown is one of its top tourist attractions.

The city's jewel-like setting on the hilly tip of a peninsula, surrounded on one side by the Pacific and on the other by San Francisco Bay ("The Bay"), one of the world's largest natural harbors, has lent it much of its appeal, for it is so undulating that the vistas are unparalleled. The streets are as unconventional as the people who live in them – sloping at 31.5° angles, twisting, tunnelling, turning into steps or dead-ending in leafy cul-de-sacs. But the dream city does have faults; in fact it sits on a very big one, the San Andreas Fault. And that does mean the city is vulnerable to earthquakes and always has been since the big one of 1906. On 17 October 1989 disaster struck again, caving in a portion of the Oakland Bay Bridge, leaving thousands homeless and causing damage which will take some years and much money to repair. But this should not deter visitors. Building techniques are such that many structures are referred to as "earthquake proof" (most of the city and all its skyscrapers survived).

So, discounting earthquakes, what has San Francisco to offer? A compact area spread over 40 hills and full of colorful neighborhoods such as the Mission District (very Latin American), North Beach (very Italian) and Fisherman's Wharf (the best of the waterfront); skyrooms (food with a view) and gingerbread houses or "Painted Ladies" (revamped Victoriana); boat trips (cruise and ferry) and charmingly rural environs (Marin County and Napa Valley); districts that are postcard pretty and districts that are downright seedy.

Above all, you have a vibrant multinational population that enjoys entertaining its visitors and making them feel at home.

Neogothic and modern jostle for space in a corner of this most idiosyncratic of American cities

BACKGROUND

California, all virgin land and redwoods, was populated by Native Americans long before the time of the first Spanish settlements in the 18th century. Although the "discovery" of this part of the world is generally credited to the Spanish in the 16th century, in fact it took them many years to travel much north of what is now San Diego. Meanwhile, Sir Francis Drake happened upon a bay along the upper Californian coast, but it is unlikely it was the one we know as San Francisco today.

City Beginnings

It was not until the Spanish realized there was a real threat from encroaching British and Russians that they got serious about actual settlements, and in 1769 an army expedition set out on what would result in a string of missions established by the Franciscan order. It could be said, therefore, that San Francisco's history only started with the founding of the Mission San Francisco de Asis (better known now as Mission Dolores) in 1776 at the cove then known as Yerba Buena (literally "good grass"). It was not the only mission to be set up around the bay. To protect their interests, the Spanish instigated those of San José, Santa Clara, San Rafael and San Francisco de Solano at Sonoma. Ranches emerged between them and by 1835 they formed a thin line of settlement. The first real settler on the cove of Yerba Buena, however, was an Englishman named William Richardson, who in 1835 chose

the site as beneficial for trading. The Russians had already set up Fort Ross in 1812 for trading purposes (furs for their Alaskan settlements) and the Americans were not slow to swell their numbers.

Although the 1846-8 war between the US and Mexico disrupted the fur trade, it was within this period that San Francisco received its official name and suddenly found itself larger than a shantytown with 150 occupants. By 1849, there were 1,000 in residence. It was the finding of gold that brought droves of newcomers, the "forty-niners," to the West, including a mass of Chinese immigrants to work in the mines and later on the railroads. San Francisco boomed, yet even in 1850 no one expected to stay for very long. The 36,000 new immigrants who arrived that year would be faced with social unrest resulting from several factors. There were too many men and not enough women and too many foreigners to suit the local preference. There was too

BACKGROUND

little law and order and the buildings were too makeshift (not to mention a fire hazard) for permanence. San Francisco had plenty of people but the communities were split: Happy Valley looked like a tented campsite; Pleasant Valley opened on to a beachfront from the center of town; and Sydney Town around Telegraph Hill was a criminals' hangout. There was already a little Chinatown full of opium dens and brothels on Upper Sacramento Street and along Dupont Street. Despite the Vigilantes, who in their pursuit of justice were not always fair-minded, and despite a number of fires like the disastrous one of 1851, San Francisco gradually rid itself of its muddy, shantytown image between 1850 and 1870, and

once the Gold Rush was down to a trickle, those who turned to banking and fishing found new futures. The city became a tuna-packing center and, as today, a banking and insurance center.

It was still the era for making money…and forward thinking could make you more. It was merchants, not miners who founded the Central Railroad Company – Leland Stanford, a grocer; Collis Huntington and Mark Hopkins, partners in the hardware trade; and, later, dry goods store owner, Charles Crocker. The quartet, all in their late thirties or forties when the company was formed, became the Big Four who were to build

California was a magnet for gold-panning fortune-hunters in 1849

mansions on Nob Hill, lay the foundations for future art galleries and lend their names to posterity. The Central Pacific Railway was completed with a last spoke in San Francisco in 1869, and the Big Four went on to the bigger and better things that a greater railway network could bestow.

When you stay at the Mark Hopkins Hotel or the Stouffer Stanford Court (both of which are situated on Nob Hill) these days you might spare a thought for these two moguls. Hopkins used to live in a small cottage on Leavenworth Street, at the foot of the hill, until his wife urged him to purchase this plusher site in 1874, when a turreted baroque castle was built. Hopkins, however, never lived to see it completed. Stanford also liked the imposing position on the hill and finished appointing his luxurious residence in 1876, surrounding his then two-acre estate with a high wall.

Nor was it the original Gold Rush which made millions for the likes of Sutro, Mackay, Flood and Fair, but findings of gold and silver much later at Comstock in Nevada. The Comstock Lode's key year was 1877 when it produced almost $50 million. After it panned out in 1880 the miners returned to San Francisco and entered new fields of interest.

Gold, however, was the original reason for the development of transportation, starting with the stage coach. Once the Rush was over there were other goods and large numbers of people requiring transportation, hence the Big Four's launch of the railway service. The latter did a great deal for the area's agriculture, providing new markets for the fruits and nuts grown in this part of the US.

Modern Times

Not all the 19th-century immigrants, however, worked on the railway. Hungarian-born Count Agoston Harászthy created a vineyard at Sonoma in 1851, where he introduced Zinfandel grapes. From that time on, Buena Vista has been a reputable name among wine-lovers. Others got the message and by the mid-1880s wine production was a lucrative and fashionable business. Indeed, everything about San Francisco was fashionable. There was plenty of music and theater, hotels and good food. The city had acquired a name both for the arts and for gold-plated service. Progress had its setbacks (six devastating fires hit the city during its boom years), and one event which stands out was the devastating earthquake and fire of 1906 which ruined much of the city, as the quake broke water mains, rendering fire-fighting equipment virtually useless – even brick buildings were destroyed. These days you will hear the term "earthquake proof" when the locals talk of their new high-rises, technical expertise which did not exist in 1906. Most disasters seem to have a bright side, though. For San Francisco, this one acted as the incentive to build a better, more beautiful city.

Part of that rebuilding program

BACKGROUND

included a cable car system. Much loved by the local populace and even more by visitors, the cable cars have became a San Francisco trademark. These days only three lines operate, more for reasons of tradition than as an economical alternative mode of getting around.

In the 1920s and 1930s San Francisco became a metropolis. There was greater use of the car, with Van Ness becoming an area of car dealers. The Bay bridges were built and the Golden Gate Park improved. All the industries connected with the waterfront flourished, and conservation took on a new importance. The city survived the Depression and World War II. Indeed, it was where 46 nations met at the end of the war to sign the UN Charter. In the last 45 years San Francisco has not been without its ups and downs. Its 1960s dose of flower power left the Haight Ashbury district distinctly branded as hippydom. The hippies have gone, but their colorful ideas have been revived by new middle-class residents who have painted the Victorian houses in bright colors and exquisite detail to create so-called Painted Ladies. An influx of more Asians has increased the Far East influence (now there is a Japantown and a plethora of Vietnamese restaurants), New skyscrapers have mushroomed, new shopping centers like Pier 39 are vying with those more established. And a large gay community that is generally well accepted has emerged in the city.

Sometimes it is hard to believe that San Francisco, so much celebrated in song, is scarcely 150 years old. As one of the city newspaper editors once said, "So much has happened in San Francisco, so fast, and only a short while ago."

Pier 39 is a favorite area for shopping, eating and family entertainment

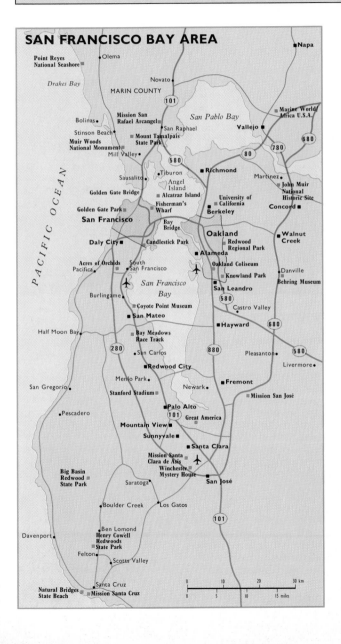

SAN FRANCISCO BAY AREA

Point Reyes National Seashore
Olema
Drakes Bay
Novato
MARIN COUNTY
101
San Pablo Bay
Napa
Marine World Africa U.S.A.
Bolinas
Mission San Rafael Arcangel
San Raphael
Vallejo
680
Stinson Beach
Mount Tamalpais State Park
780
Muir Woods National Monument
Mill Valley
80
580
Richmond
Martinez
John Muir National Historic Site
Sausalito
Tiburon
Angel Island
Alcatraz Island
University of California
Concord
PACIFIC OCEAN
Golden Gate Bridge
Fisherman's Wharf
Berkeley
Golden Gate Park
Bay Bridge
Oakland
Walnut Creek
San Francisco
Daly City
Candlestick Park
Redwood Regional Park
Acres of Orchids
South San Francisco
Alameda
Oakland Coliseum
Danville
Behring Museum
Pacifica
San Francisco Bay
Knowland Park
Burlingame
Coyote Point Museum
San Leandro
580
San Mateo
Castro Valley
Half Moon Bay
Bay Meadows Race Track
Hayward
680
280
San Carlos
880
Pleasanton
580
Redwood City
Livermore
Menlo Park
Fremont
San Gregorio
Stanford Stadium
Newark
Mission San José
Pescadero
Palo Alto
101
Great America
Mountain View
Sunnyvale
Santa Clara
Mission Santa Clara de Asis
Winchester Mystery House
San José
Big Basin Redwood State Park
Saratoga
Boulder Creek
Los Gatos
101
Davenport
Ben Lomond
Henry Cowell Redwoods State Park
Felton
Scotts Valley
Natural Bridges State Beach
Santa Cruz
Mission Santa Cruz

0   10   20   30 km
0   5   10   15 miles

CHURCHES AND TEMPLES

WHAT TO SEE

Churches and Temples

◆
BUDDHA'S UNIVERSAL CHURCH
Chinatown at Washington and Kearny Streets
One of the largest Buddhist churches in the US, if not *the* largest, it was built by volunteers of the Pristine Orthodox Dharma and completed in 1961. A *bodhi* tree, grown from a slip of the one under which Buddha is said to have found enlightenment over 2,500 years ago, graces the roof beside a lotus pool. A bilingual play is given in national dress here on weekends, January to March.
Open: second and fourth Sunday in each month from 1:00–2:30P.M..

Grace Cathedral, one of the most impressive gothic buildings in the US

◆
GRACE CATHEDRAL
California and Taylor Streets, on Nob Hill
One of the finest examples of gothic architecture in the US, this is the country's third largest Episcopal cathedral. Built in 1928, it is the seat of the Episcopal Bishop of California. Note the doors at the east entrance which are replicas of the Ghiberti originals in the Florence Baptistry. The cathedral is on the site of a former mansion belonging to Charles Crocker, one of the Big Four.
Open: daily 7:30A.M.–6:00P.M. (6:30P.M. Thursday). Tours 1:00–3:00P.M. (except Monday, 10:00A.M.–noon). Free.
For information call 776-6611.

◆
KONG CHOW TEMPLE
Clay and Stockton Streets
Kong Chow is Chinatown's oldest
family association, formerly
located at Pine and Kearny. The
temple, on the fourth floor of a
new building, houses many old
artifacts.
Open: daily 9:00A.M.–4:00P.M..
Donation requested.
For information call 434-2513.

◆◆◆
MISSION DOLORES
16th and Dolores Streets
Properly called Mission San
Francisco de Asis, it takes its
popular name from a lake that
used to exist nearby – Laguna de
Nuestra Señora de los Dolores
(Lake of Our Lady of Sorrows). It
was the sixth of the string of 21
missions established by the
Franciscans. The mission was
founded in 1776, and the mission
building is thought to be the
city's oldest structure. Of
particular note are its thick
adobe walls and its hewn timber
roof lashed together with
rawhide. It was here that
California's first book, a life of the
founding father Junípero Serra,
was written. The architectural
style of the mission's church is a
mixture of Moorish, ''Mission''
and Corinthian elements with an
altar and decorations from Spain
and Mexico. Many early
pioneers are buried in the
cemetery alongside. A small
museum contains old
manuscripts and artifacts.
Open: daily 9:00A.M.–4:00P.M.
(until 4:30P.M. in summer).
No admission charge but
donation requested.
For information call 621-8203.

OLD ST MARY'S CHURCH (see
Landmarks and Monuments,
page 27).

◆
ST MARY'S CATHEDRAL
Geary and Gough Streets
A strikingly modern Catholic
cathedral atop Cathedral Hill,
built to replace the original St
Mary's destroyed by a fire in
1962. Constructed in Italian
travertine and approached via
brick plazas, the cathedral's
interior features enormous
stained-glass windows and a
most unusual free-form structure
above the altar that symbolizes
prayer and divine grace. Self-
guided tours.
Open: daily 6:45A.M.–5:00P.M..
For information call 567-2020.

◆
TIEN HOU TEMPLE
125 Waverly Place (4th floor)
A Chinatown temple dedicated
to Tien Hou, Queen of Heaven,
and erected in thanks for the
safe arrival of Chinese
immigrants in 1852.
Open: daily 10:00A.M.–4:00P.M..
For information call 391-4841.

Districts

◆◆
ALAMO SQUARE
at Hayes and Steiner Streets
One of several now designated
historic districts, the area
embraces some classic
Victorian buildings, many of
which have been converted into
charming little bed and
breakfast inns; the Imperial
Russian consulate of Tsarist
days; and a 1904 archbishop's
castle.

◆ CASTRO DISTRICT

The Eureka Valley section of Upper Market Street near Castro Street has recently been revitalized, with the planting of magnolia trees and the conversion of 1880s Victorian buildings into boutiques, bookstores and pubs just steps away from the Muni station. This is a gay section of town with gay bars and restaurants and gay-owned and -patronized businesses. This district was represented by slain councilman Harvey Milk who was openly gay.

Chinatown, once a byword for vice, is now a tourist attraction

CHINATOWN

Grant Avenue, between Bush Street and Broadway
A teeming and colorful city-within-a-city, whose hub is an eight-block belt along Grant Avenue. It is the largest Chinese community outside Asia – a labyrinth of Asian shops, restaurants, tearooms, markets, theaters and temples. You can't miss finding it, for the roofs are pagoda-shaped and the lamp posts entwined by dragons. Dragons and stone lions adorn the Gateway to Chinatown (at Grant and Bush Streets), a green and gold arch erected in 1970.

EMBARCADERO

The Embarcadero is that stretch of waterfront east of Fisherman's Wharf – the port. Here, at the foot of Market Street the **Ferry Building**, housing the World Trade Center (and also the San Francisco Port Commission), has long been an Embarcadero landmark. To the south is the terminal for the Golden Gate ferries to Marin County. From the Ferry Building to the base of the Oakland Bridge runs the waterfront promenade, ideal for joggers or for those who like to fish or just admire the view. The major attraction of the Embarcadero area is the Embarcadero Center (see **Shopping**, page 84).

FINANCIAL DISTRICT

north and south of Market Street, from Kearny to the Embarcadero
California's answer to Wall Street, this district, focusing on

Montgomery Street, is where you will find all the major banks and insurance company headquarters as well as stockbrokers. A number of them are landmarks like the tallest structure, the **Transamerica Pyramid**, the 853-foot (260m) earthquake-proof wedge at 600 Montgomery Street, conceived as a corporate symbol. Almost as tall is the impressive, carnelian marble clad 779-foot (237.5m) **Bank of America World Headquarters Building** at 555 California Street. Then comes the 724-foot (220.5m) **First Interstate Center** at 345 California Street, capped by twin turrets which link 11 floors of glass skybridges. Note, too, that **Crown Zellerbach** at 1 Bush Street was the first San Francisco building with a plaza (though many have them now), and that the open courtyard of the **Citicorp Tower** at 1 Sansome Street is graced by the "Star Girl" figure dating from the 1915 Panama-Pacific Exposition.

◆◆◆
FISHERMAN'S WHARF
Jefferson and Taylor Streets, east and west along the waterfront
Everyone's favorite area, brimming with fishing boats, net-menders, seafood stalls, bakeries selling delicious sourdough bread, souvenir shops and museums. It is just the place to sample crab, indoors or out, fresh during the mid-November to June season; and just the place to be on the first Sunday in October when the annual Blessing of the Fishing Fleet

The harbor at Fisherman's Wharf

takes place. Fisherman's Wharf is easy to reach: two of the cable car lines terminate here and many of the sight-seeing boats leave from Piers 39 and 41.

◆
JACKSON SQUARE
Jackson Street, from Montgomery Street to Battery Street
This six-block historic district is a redeveloped version of what was a boozy, brawling quarter – the original Barbary Coast. The Jackson-Montgomery corner was the site of the city's first bridge built over a backwater in 1844 to act as a shortcut to the nearby bayfront. The crossroads by that bridge became known as "Murderer's Corner." Many buildings you can still see today survived the 1906 quake and fire (which left 2,000 dead), but as the city was rebuilt and the waterfront edged eastward to its present point, those 19th-century buildings became "has-beens." It was not until the 1950s that "new pioneers"

16

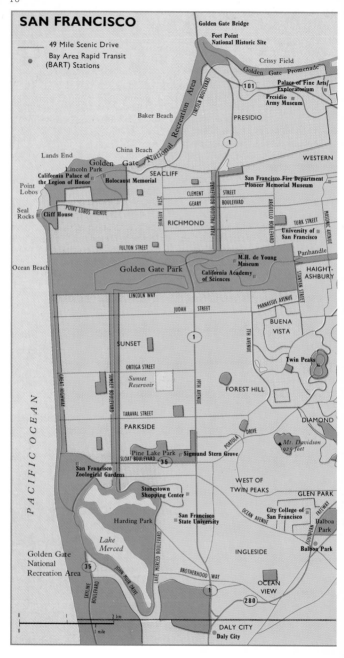

SAN FRANCISCO

— 49 Mile Scenic Drive

● Bay Area Rapid Transit (BART) Stations

Golden Gate Bridge
Fort Point National Historic Site
Crissy Field
Golden Gate Promenade
Palace of Fine Arts/ Exploratorium
Presidio Army Museum
PRESIDIO
Baker Beach
China Beach
WESTERN
Lands End
Golden Gate National Recreation Area
SEACLIFF
California Palace of the Legion of Honor
Holocaust Memorial
San Francisco Fire Department Pioneer Memorial Museum
Point Lobos
CLEMENT STREET
GEARY BOULEVARD
Seal Rocks Cliff House
POINT LOBOS AVENUE
RICHMOND
TURK STREET
University of San Francisco
FULTON STREET
Panhandle
Ocean Beach
Golden Gate Park
M.H. de Young Museum
California Academy of Sciences
HAIGHT-ASHBURY
LINCOLN WAY
JUDAH STREET
PARNASSUS AVENUE
BUENA VISTA
SUNSET
Twin Peaks
ORTEGA STREET
Sunset Reservoir
FOREST HILL
TARAVAL STREET
PARKSIDE
DIAMOND
Mt. Davidson 925 feet
Pine Lake Park
Sigmund Stern Grove
SLOAT BOULEVARD
San Francisco Zoological Gardens
WEST OF TWIN PEAKS
GLEN PARK
Stonestown Shopping Center
City College of San Francisco
Balboa Park
Harding Park
San Francisco State University
OCEAN AVENUE
Balboa Park
Lake Merced
INGLESIDE
Golden Gate National Recreation Area
BROTHERHOOD WAY
OCEAN VIEW
PACIFIC OCEAN
DALY CITY
Daly City

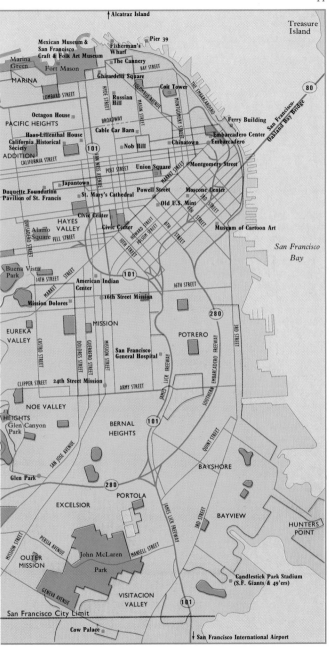

↑ Alcatraz Island

Treasure Island

Pier 39

Fisherman's Wharf

Mexican Museum & San Francisco Craft & Folk Art Museum

The Cannery

Marina Green

Fort Mason

Ghirardelli Square

MARINA

Coit Tower

LOMBARD STREET

Russian Hill

PACIFIC HEIGHTS

Octagon House

BROADWAY

Ferry Building

Haas-Lilienthal House

Cable Car Barn

Embarcadero Center

California Historical Society

Nob Hill

Chinatown

Embarcadero

San Francisco-Oakland Bay Bridge

ADDITION

CALIFORNIA STREET

POST STREET

Union Square

Montgomery Street

Japantown

Duquette Foundation Pavilion of St. Francis

St. Mary's Cathedral

Powell Street

Moscone Center

Old U.S. Mint

HAYES VALLEY

Civic Center

Civic Center

Alamo Square

FELL STREET

HOWARD STREET

Museum of Cartoon Art

San Francisco Bay

Buena Vista Park

14TH STREET

MARKET

American Indian Center

16TH STREET

Mission Dolores

16th Street Mission

EUREKA VALLEY

MISSION

POTRERO

CASTRO STREET

San Francisco General Hospital

CLIPPER STREET

24th Street Mission

ARMY STREET

NOE VALLEY

HEIGHTS

Glen Canyon Park

BERNAL HEIGHTS

SAN JOSE AVENUE

QUINT STREET

Glen Park

BAYSHORE

PORTOLA

EXCELSIOR

BAYVIEW

HUNTERS POINT

PERSIA AVENUE

MANSELL STREET

John McLaren

OUTER MISSION

Park

Candlestick Park Stadium (S.F. Giants & 49'ers)

GENEVA AVENUE

VISITACION VALLEY

San Francisco City Limit

Cow Palace

↓ San Francisco International Airport

began refurbishing them and converting them into decorative supply showrooms. Nowadays, antique dealers and offices predominate. Jackson Street landmarks to note between Sansome and Montgomery Streets are No 400 which dates in part from 1859; 415-31, built in 1853 and used by Domingo Ghirardelli as his chocolate works prior to moving to Ghirardelli Square; No 441, erected in 1861 on the hulls of two abandoned ships; 458-60, dating from 1854; 470, built in 1852 and used to house the consulates of Spain and Chile and, later, France; and No 472, constructed in 1850 using ship masts as interior supporting columns, and also, in the last century, the site of the French consulate.

◆
JAPANTOWN
Japan Center at Geary Boulevard, Fillmore Street, Post Street, Laguna Street and adjacent areas

Citizens of Japanese descent call it Nihonmachi or Japantown, and its focal point is a huge complex of shops and showrooms, Japanese baths, cafés and bars. Peace Plaza here, crowned by a five-tier pagoda (a gift from the Japanese) is the setting for ethnic festivals like the April Cherry Blossom Festival.
To reach this part of town take a 38 bus (Geary) or a 2, 3 or 4 on Sutter westbound to Laguna. (See also **Shopping**, page 85.)

Painted Ladies, restored Victorian houses, adorn Mission District

MISSION DISTRICT
A bustling business and residential area whose majority of occupants are Spanish speaking, its main thoroughfare, Mission Street, once connected the Mission San Francisco de Asis (Mission Dolores) to the Presidio. The first Levi Strauss factory was located in this district and is still in use at 250 Valencia Street. Some of the gaily painted Victorian houses known as Painted Ladies are to be seen in the Mission District streets. Easily reached via BART (Bay Area Rapid Transit) to the 24th Street station or by taking the southbound 14 bus on Mission Street from downtown.

NOB HILL
around California, Sacramento, Jones and Taylor Streets
In the Gold Rush era this was a fashionable residential district for wealthy citizens (*nabos* – nobs). Today it is an elegant area for the well-to-do to stay. In addition to exclusive hotels this is the area of the Pacific Union Club, the California Masonic Memorial Temple, Grace Cathedral and Huntington Park.

NORTH BEACH
The northeast section of the city spread around Telegraph Hill, with Columbus Avenue as its main artery, this area gets its name from the 1850s era when a finger of the Bay extended inland and this indeed was a shoreline neighborhood. Today North Beach has a vibrant Italian-influenced nightlife with numerous cabarets, coffee houses, bistros with music, jazz clubs and delis brimming with *prosciutto* and *provolone*. A popular brown bag lunch spot is Washington Square.

PACIFIC HEIGHTS
This is San Francisco's most exclusive residential quarter, a parade of great mansions with beautifully painted façades. The best browsing area is along the Broadway bluff between Webster and Lyon Streets. Note the Hamlin School at 2120 Broadway and the Convent of the Sacred Heart at 2222 Broadway; also the Spreckels Mansion at 2080 Washington Street, the Whittier Mansion at 2090 Jackson Street and the Bourn Mansion at 2550 Webster Street. Make a stop where Broderick Street crosses Broadway for a good view of the Marina district, Palace of Fine Arts, the Golden Gate Bridge and Marin County beyond.

◆
RUSSIAN HILL
between Nob Hill and Fisherman's Wharf
This district of lanes and terraces takes its name from the Russian seal hunters who were active in the early 1800s in local waters. Today Russian Hill is a prestigious address.

UNION SQUARE
Powell, Stockton, Geary and Post Streets
Heart of the shopping district and site of many civic events. The monument in the center commemorates Admiral George Dewey's victory over the Spanish at Manila Bay in 1898.

Historic Buildings and Ships

San Francisco's maritime history is featured in popular Aquatic Park

◆◆◆
BALCLUTHA
Pier 43, Fisherman's Wharf
A historic triple-masted square-rigged vessel which made her maiden voyage around the Horn in 1887, now a permanent exhibit as part of the National Maritime Museum (see page 36).
Open: daily 10:00A.M.–6:00P.M. (5:00P.M. in winter). Admission charge (ages 17-61) includes viewing other historic boats at Hyde Street Pier (see page 21).

CONSERVATORY OF FLOWERS
(see **Landmarks and Monuments**, page 25).

◆
HAAS-LILIENTHAL HOUSE
2007 Franklin Street at Jackson Street
Survivor of the 1906 earthquake, this handsome Queen Anne-style mansion, built in 1886, is an excellent representative of those fashionable homes which flourished in the Victorian era. Maintained by the Foundation for San Francisco's Architectural Heritage, its ornamental façade and interior floor plan exemplify all such houses of the period.
Open for tours: Wednesday noon–4:00P.M. (last tour 3:15P.M.), Sunday 11:00A.M.–4:15P.M. (last tour 4:00P.M.). Admission charge (under-12s and seniors half price). For information call 441-3004.

◆◆◆
HYDE STREET PIER
foot of Hyde Street, between Fisherman's Wharf and Aquatic Park
This is part of the National

Maritime Museum (see page 36). The six restored historic vessels moored at this pier include the *CA Thayer,* a three-masted 1895 schooner typical of the kind which used to carry timber. The *Wapama* is a 1915 wooden steamer which carried both timber and passengers between Pacific coastal ports, while the paddle-wheel ferry boat *Eureka* spent most of her time in San Francisco Bay. *Alma* is a scow schooner, also once a Bay working boat, carrying hay and other cargoes, such as building materials and grain. The *Hercules* is a good example of a US steam tug which operated between 1907 and 1962. Favourite is *Balclutha* (see page 20). Self-guided or ranger-led tours are offered.
Open: daily 10:00A.M.–6:00P.M. (5:00P.M. in winter). Admission charge but under-17s and seniors free. For information call 556-6435.

SS *JEREMIAH O'BRIEN*
Fort Mason Center, Pier 3 East, Marina Boulevard and Buchanan Street
America's last Liberty Ship, one of the great fleet that operated in World War II, remains in operating condition at Fort Mason, having been restored by dedicated volunteers. Best time to visit is on an Open Ship weekend (generally the third weekend of the month, except May and December, but call 441-3101 to verify dates) when the ship's triple expansion steam engine is working, the coal stove galley is open and the "Slop Chest" store is set up. During the third

weekend in May, the *Jeremiah O'Brien* conducts cruises of the Bay (passengers welcome).
Open: daily 9:00A.M.–3:00P.M.; weekends 11:00A.M.–4:00P.M.. Admission charge (extra during Open Ship weekends).

♦
OCTAGON HOUSE
2645 Gough Street at Union Street
A unique building furnished in Colonial and Federal style, the house was built in 1861. It is an early San Franciscan residence, one of two remaining examples of octagonal designs, and was purchased this century by the National Society of Colonial Dames of America in California.
Open: second and fourth Thursday and second Sunday of each month (except January) from noon–3:00P.M.. Donations. For information call 441-7512.

OLD US MINT
Fifth and Mission Streets
Architecturally this 1873 building is referred to as "Federal Classical Revival." It contains several authentically restored rooms, including the notable Mint Director's Office. The highlight is the circular vault where a pyramid of gold bars valued at $5 million is displayed, but other features include the collection of privately minted coins, ore and metal exhibits and artworks. The striking of one's own souvenir medal on an 1869 press is popular with tourists.
Open: Monday to Friday 10:00A.M.–4:00P.M.. Free tours, starting on the hour (last tour 3:00P.M.). For information call 744-6830.

HISTORIC BUILDINGS AND SHIPS/LANDMARKS

USS *PAMPANITO*
Pier 45, Fisherman's Wharf, at end of Taylor Street
This 312-foot (95m) submarine saw a great deal of action in World War II. It has since been renovated and may be toured – an audio tour system provides an informative commentary.
Open: daily 9:00A.M.–9:00P.M., except Sunday to Thursday from mid-October to mid-May when opening hours are 9:00A.M.–6:00P.M. (Friday and Saturday 9:00A.M.–9:00P.M.). Admission charge (under-5s free).
For information call 929-0202.

◆

WHITTIER MANSION
2090 Jackson Street at Laguna Street
The 1896 mansion houses the California Historical Society. It is a prime example of the type of opulent home that the wealthy lived in at the turn of the century, with some beautiful furniture and fixtures of the era in period rooms. The Fine Arts Collection, especially, reflects the lifestyle of early Californians, drawing a vivid picture of how the state developed from its beginnings through 1906. The rare lithographs, watercolors, oil paintings, drawings and artifacts are displayed on a rotating basis so that even the second- or third-time visitor may discover something not seen before. The Society also maintains a research/reference center around the corner on Pacific Avenue.

Open: Tuesday to Saturday 1:00–4:30P.M., with guided tours at 1:30P.M., and also at 3:00P.M. on weekends. Admission charge except on first Wednesday of each month. For more information call 567-1848.

Landmarks and Monuments

CIVIC CENTER
Van Ness Avenue, Market Street and Golden Gate triangle
The city's civic pride is reflected in this monumental complex, spread over eight blocks, which is one of the largest in the US.
City Hall has a grand French Renaissance look about it and a dome taller than Washington's. It was completed in 1915 and its handsome staircase, rotunda and marble corridors are an impressive office base for over 1,200 employees. It is one of eight buildings clustered around Civic Center Plaza, forming the nucleus for all the city's and county's civil services.
Civic Auditorium, seating over 7,000 is the scene of numerous cultural and sports events and conventions and has two adjoining halls, each with seating for an additional 900 people. Beneath the Plaza is **Brooks Exhibit Hall**, added in 1958. Nearby stands the **Main Library**, a Beaux Arts structure that houses over a million books, several special collections and the **San Francisco History Room** (see page 37), where old maps, photographs, newspapers and other documents are catalogued. There are special displays, too, on the history of the city's police department along with

San Franciscans' pride in their city is reflected in the grand City Hall

household items salvaged from the 1906 earthquake. Not far from the library are the Federal Building, the Federal Office Building, the State Office Building and the Public Utilities Commission headquarters. Opposite City Hall is the **San Francisco War Memorial** and **Performing Arts Center,** comprising the $27.5 million Louise M Davies Symphony Hall, the War Memorial Opera House, the Veteran's Memorial Building and the Ballet Building. The Veteran's Memorial Building contains the Herbst Theater and the **Museum of Modern Art** (see page 35). Together they form one of the US's largest and most impressive arts complexes. In front of the Louise M Davies Hall

is Henry Moore's sculpture *Large Four Piece Reclining Figure.* The hall itself is home to one of the country's oldest symphony orchestras, founded in 1911, and is designed with seating that makes you feel close to the action, including that behind the orchestra. The **War Memorial Opera House** is the home stage for San Francisco's own Opera founded in 1923 and the San Francisco Ballet, founded 10 years later. The adjacent **Herbst Theater** was the site chosen for the signing of the United Nations Charter in 1945 and is decorated with murals by the British painter Frank Brangwyn.
Open: for tours on Monday 10:00A.M.–2:30P.M. on every half hour but tours of Davies Hall only on Wednesday at 1:30 and 2:30P.M. and on Saturday at 12:30 and 1:30P.M.. Admission charge.

LANDMARKS

For reservations call 552-8338.
Tours begin from the Grove
Street entrance of Davies Hall.

◆◆
CLIFF HOUSE
1066 to 1090 Point Lobos Avenue
It was here at Ocean Beach that
Adolph Sutro, inventor of a
sophisticated gold mining
process, created an elaborate
resort in the late 1890s, which he
opened to the public. He became
mayor in 1895 and opened Cliff
House the following year. The
building you see today – a
restaurant and cocktail lounge
complex – built in 1909, is the
third to stand on its cliff-top site,
but the view of Seal Rocks and
the ocean below is worth the
price of a drink.
By taking the 38L-Geary bus on
weekdays or the 38-Geary
marked 48th Avenue on
evenings or weekends, you will

reach Point Lobos.
For information call 386-3330.

◆◆
COIT TOWER
*Telegraph Hill, at the eastern end
of Lombard Street*
Telegraph Hill takes its name
from the days when a
semaphore was used to signal
the approach of ships through
the Golden Gate. Its position,
overlooking the north and east
Bay attracted artists and at one
time it was simply known as the
Art Colony. Today it is a
fashionable residential district
with cottages and apartment
buildings. To reach Telegraph
Hill take the No 39 bus from
Washington Square.
Capping the hill is **Pioneer Park**
where a bronze statue of

*Telegraph Hill, topped by Coit Tower,
rising to the east of Leavenworth*

Christopher Columbus stands, but right at the summit is the most salient feature – the strange cylinder that is Coit Tower. This is the legacy of Lillie Hitchcock Coit who left a $125,000 bequest "for the purpose of adding beauty to the city I have always loved." The tower was erected in 1933 and its rotunda is filled with murals representing the hill's artistic zenith. The main reason for tourists to come here is to take the elevator to the 210-foot (64m) high observation platform for the superb view, with the Bay stretched out 542 feet (165m) below.
Open: daily 9:00A.M.–4:30P.M. (from 10:00A.M.–5:30P.M. March to September). Admission charge but under-sixes go free.
For information call 274-0203.

◆
CONSERVATORY OF FLOWERS
Golden Gate Park (northeast corner) on John F Kennedy Drive
This, the oldest building in the park (see page 41), is a supreme example of Victorian architecture. A James Lick purchased the property in England, then had it shipped to San Francisco via Cape Horn and reconstructed in its original form in 1879. Today it is listed on the National Register of Historic Places. Two floral plaques fronting the building are constantly changed to portray current events and special themes.
Open: daily 9:00A.M.–6:00P.M. (to 5:00P.M. November to March). Admission charge, but under-12s free.
For information call 558-3973.

◆◆
FORT MASON
Bay and Franklin Streets, Laguna Street and Marina Boulevard (Piers 2 and 3)
Today this former military installation and port of embarkation is the headquarters for the Golden Gate National Recreation Area. All kinds of lively events take place in this area, from exhibitions to food fairs and concerts – around 1,000 activities each month. Some of the buildings house resident theaters and performing arts groups and there are galleries, restaurants and coffee houses. The SS *Jeremiah O'Brien* is berthed at Pier 3 (see page 21). Maps and activity listings can be picked up at the Park Headquarters Building, open 9:00A.M. to 5:00P.M., Monday to Friday.
To reach Fort Mason take the northbound 30 bus, Stockton to Chestnut and Laguna, then the northbound 28 on Laguna, or walk the four blocks remaining. Call 441-5706 for information.

◆◆
FORT POINT NATIONAL HISTORIC SITE
Presidio via Lincoln Boulevard to Long Avenue
This classic example of brick forts built by US army engineers is located at the base of the south tower of the Golden Gate Bridge. Completed in 1861 the four-tiered structure once housed 146 cannon (none of which was ever fired in anger) and 600 soldiers. Nowadays, National Park Service guides in Civil War uniforms conduct free tours of the fort, including

cannon-loading demonstrations.
Open: daily 10:00A.M.–5:00P.M..
Free.
For information call 556-1693.

◆◆◆
GOLDEN GATE BRIDGE
entrance to San Francisco Bay
Not golden at all but a rusty red,
constantly maintained by a crew
of painters, the bridge is a
magnificent span, almost a piece
of artwork and certainly a
masterly engineering
achievement. They used to call it
"the bridge that couldn't be
built," but built it was, opening in
1937 to become San Francisco's
most photographed landmark.

*One of the world's most beautiful
structures – Golden Gate Bridge*

It took designer Joseph Strauss
13 years to get an OK for its
construction and it remains one
of the world's longest suspension
bridges, measuring 6,450 feet
(1,966m), to link the city with
Marin County and beyond.
The cost, huge for the time, was
$35 million. There is a toll for
southbound cars but northbound
drivers and cyclists and
pedestrians may cross free. One
of the best viewpoints is at Vista
Point on the northern approach,
where you can have an eye-level
look at the 36½-inch (93cm)

painted in a white patina, was commissioned by a citizens' committee, created by American sculptor George Segal and dedicated in 1984.

◆

JUSTIN HERMAN PLAZA
foot of Market Street
All the street action – artists, merchants, theater – can be seen in this large landscaped urban area across from the Ferry Building (see page 14). The plaza's main feature is **Vaillancourt Fountain**, a giant free-form sculpture designed as a "walk through."

◆◆◆
LOMBARD STREET
You must drive down it at least once! It is often referred to as the crookedest street in the world – a descent of Russian Hill in nine hairpin bends on the one block between Hyde and Leavenworth Streets. Stairs are available for pedestrians to climb the 40° slope.

◆
OLD ST MARY'S CHURCH
California Street and Grant Avenue (Chinatown)
This church was erected in 1854 and survived both the 1906 fire and the later one of 1966 so it is quite an established landmark. Above the clock dial its red brick façade bears the warning "Son Observe the Time and Fly from Evil."
You will find the city's first cathedral diagonally across from St Mary's Square where a statue of Dr Sun Yat-Sen (first president of the Chinese Republic), sculpted by Beniamino Bufano,

suspension cables. Look west and you will see the Needles, an offshore rock formation; the Lime Point Lighthouse; Horseshoe Bay; and the buildings of Fort Baker. It is an exhilarating – if sometimes breezy – experience.
To reach the bridge from downtown or Fisherman's Wharf take a northbound 30 bus, Stockton to Chestnut and Laguna, then transfer to a southbound 28 on Laguna to the Toll Plaza.

◆

HOLOCAUST MEMORIAL
corner of El Camino del Mar and Legion of Honor Drive
This outdoor bronze sculpture,

Pier 45
USS Pampanito
Hyde Street Pier   Pier 43
Pier 39
The San Francisco Experience
Balclutha
SS Jeremiah O'Brian
Fisherman's Wharf
Aquatic Park   Guinness Museum of World Records
The Cannery &   The   JEFFERSON STREET
Toy Museum   Anchorage   Enchanted World, Haunted Gold Mine,
National Maritime   BEACH STREET   Wax Museum, Ripley's Believe it or Not!
Museum   American   NORTH POINT STREET
Carousel Museum
Fort Mason   Ghirardelli
Square   THE EMBARCADERO
BAY STREET   BAY STREET
BAY STREET   Russian Hill   TELEGRAPH
Park   COLUMBUS AVENUE   HILL
Lombard Street Hill   MASON STREET   Coit Tower
LOMBARD STREET   Crookedest Street   LOMBARD STREET   Pioneer Park
FRANKLIN STREET   STOCKTON STREET   FILBERT STREET
GOUGH STREET   VAN NESS AVENUE   POLK STREET   North Beach   GRANT AVENUE
LOMBARD STREET   Playground   Washington   UNION STREET   BATTERY STREET
UNION STREET   HYDE STREET   Square   SANSOME STREET
UNION STREET   LEAVENWORTH STREET   NORTH   COLUMBUS AVENUE
BEACH   POWELL STREET   California Historical
TAYLOR STREET   BROADWAY   Society of America
PACIFIC   Jackson
HEIGHTS   BROADWAY   Tunnel   Chinese   Square
Haas-Lilienthal   RUSSIAN HILL   Tien-Hou   Culture   Transamerica
House   JACKSON STREET   Temple   Center   Pyramid
Cable Car Barn   Kong Chow   Portsmouth   MONTGOMERY STREET   CLAY STREET
Lafayette   WASHINGTON STREET   Temple   Square   Wells
Park   CLAY STREET   Huntington   CHINATOWN   Fargo
POLK STREET   Grace Cathedral   Park   Old   CALIFORNIA STREET   Museum
CALIFORNIA STREET   St. Mary's   KEARNY STREET   Bank of
NOB HILL   Church   America
GOUGH STREET   Masonic   PINE STREET   World
PINE STREET   HYDE STREET   Auditorium   Headquarters
St. Francis   BUSH STREET   Chinatown   Crocker
BUSH STREET   Memorial Hospital   TAYLOR STREET   Gateway   Galleria
MASON STREET   POST STREET
VAN NESS AVENUE   Union GEARY STREET   Montgomery
POST STREET   Square   Street
Japantown   GEARY STREET   Geary Theater   MISSION STREET
GEARY BOULEVARD   LEAVENWORTH STREET   Museum of   3RD STREET
St. Mary's   O'FARRELL STREET   Airport Bus Terminal   Modern Mythology
Cathedral   The   San Francisco Center
Great American   Powell Street   Moscone
FRANKLIN STREET   Music Hall   POLK STREET   Convention Center
WESTERN   Federal   HYDE STREET   Old U.S. Mint   SOUTH OF
TURK STREET   Building   TURK STREET   4TH STREET
ADDITION   GOLDEN GATE AVENUE   Friends of
Pioneer Hall   Photography
State Building   State Building   Federal   MARKET
Museum of Modern Art,   MCALLISTER STREET   Building   Main Post Office   5TH STREET
Veteran's Building   City   Library   Civic
S.F. Ballet Association   Hall   Center   Greyhound   HOWARD STREET
Opera House   GROVE STREET   Bus Depot   6TH STREET   JAMES LICK SKYWAY
HAYES   Civic Center   7TH STREET   HARRISON STREET
VALLEY   HAYES STREET   Civic Auditorium   MISSION STREET
FELL STREET   Davis Symphony   VAN NESS AVENUE   8TH STREET   FOLSOM STREET
GOUGH STREET   Hall   San Francisco   9TH STREET
OAK STREET   Mart   10TH STREET
MARKET STREET

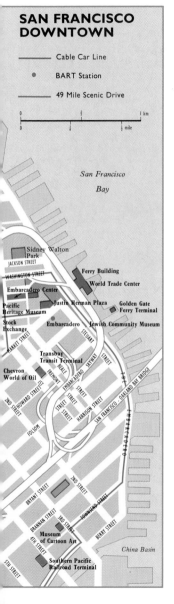

SAN FRANCISCO DOWNTOWN

—— Cable Car Line

● BART Station

—— 49 Mile Scenic Drive

San Francisco Bay

Sidney Walton Park
JACKSON STREET
WASHINGTON STREET
Embarcadero Center
Pacific Heritage Museum
Stock Exchange
Ferry Building
World Trade Center
Justin Herman Plaza
Golden Gate Ferry Terminal
Embarcadero
Jewish Community Museum
MARKET STREET
Transbay Transit Terminal
STEUART STREET
Chevron World of Oil
BEALE STREET
FREMONT STREET
EMBARCADERO SKYWAY
2ND STREET
HOWARD STREET
FOLSOM
HARRISON STREET
SAN FRANCISCO–OAKLAND BAY BRIDGE
BRYANT STREET
2ND STREET
BRANNAN STREET
3RD STREET
TOWNSEND STREET
4TH STREET
Museum of Cartoon Art
BERRY STREET
China Basin
5TH STREET
Southern Pacific Railroad Terminal

watches benignly over the senior citizens and the younger "brown baggers."
Open: Monday to Friday 9:00A.M.–5:00P.M..
Free entry.

◆◆◆
PALACE OF FINE ARTS
Marina Boulevard and Baker Street
A landmark ever since it was built in 1915 for the Panama-Pacific Exposition, restored to its original splendor in 1967 with its handsome Greco-Romanesque rotunda and Corinthian colonnades, it now houses the **Exploratorium** (see page 34). There is also a 1,000-seat theater here, where numerous cultural and entertainment events take place. The area around the palace is a park with a lagoon, home to a population of waterfowl. Easily reached by a northbound 30 bus – Stockton to Broderick and Beach.

◆
PORTSMOUTH SQUARE
Kearny Street between Clay and Washington Streets
It was here on 9 July 1846 (when San Francisco was still known as Yerba Buena) that Commander John B Montgomery landed from the sloop *Portsmouth* to claim the territory for the US and raise the American flag. The city's first schoolhouse stood here and a monument to Robert Louis Stevenson was erected in 1897. Other writers who haunted the spot were Jack London and Rudyard Kipling. Nowadays, the square is a grassy area (over an underground garage) and a meeting spot.

PRESIDIO

northwest of the city, main gate at Lombard and Lyon Streets

"Presidio" was what the Spaniards called their garrisons. This one was established in 1776 and even today the 1,500 acres (610 hectares) of wooded hills are headquarters for the United States Sixth Army; that makes this one of the oldest military stations in the country, but it is on the list of military bases scheduled to close in the next few years. The adobe Officers' Club is one of the two oldest buildings in the city, and the cannons lining the approach to the Officers' Open Mess are 300 years old. The stables of the Eighth Cavalry still stand and the old hospital is a museum (see page 37).

Museums

AMERICAN CAROUSEL MUSEUM

633 Beach Street

Here, opposite the Cannery at Fisherman's Wharf, some of the finest examples of antique carousel art carving can be seen. The exhibits of hand-carved figures and animals made between 1880 and 1930 come from New York and Philadelphia and are a valuable segment of US woodcraft heritage. Displays change quarterly and are supplemented by slides, photos, Wurlitzer and North Tonawanda band organs and workshop demonstrations on restoration techniques. Informative for adults and a delight for the small fry. The Museum will temporarily close in October 1993 but will reopen in May 1994. Call 928-0550 for further information before your visit.

ASIAN ART MUSEUM, AVERY BRUNDAGE COLLECTION

Golden Gate Park

Former International Olympics Committee president Avery Brundage chose San Francisco to house his vast collection of Oriental art treasures, and a specially constructed museum was built as a permanent showcase in the 1960s. Half of the collection is of Chinese origin and you can see this in the galleries on the main floor that radiate off the entry court. It includes some magnificent jades and Chinese blue and white porcelains. On the second floor *objets d'art* from India, Japan, Southeast Asia and the Near East are displayed.

Open: Wednesday to Sunday 10:00A.M.–5:00P.M. Admission charge generally, but under-12s free and free to all on the first Wednesday of every month (open until 8.45P.M.) and the first Saturday of the month until noon. Free tours available.

For more information call 668-8921.

BEHRING AUTO MUSEUM

3750 Blackhawk Plaza Circle, Danville

A uniquely designed museum that houses the $100 million Behring collection of classic automobiles. The cars look almost like works of art the way they are displayed under special-effect lighting within the granite galleries of a vaulted, glass-sheathed building.

Open: Tuesday to Saturday, 10:00A.M.–5:00P.M. (to 9:00P.M. Wednesday and Friday). Guided tours by reservation only. Admission charge. For more information call 736-2277.

◆◆◆
CABLE CAR MUSEUM, POWERHOUSE AND CAR BARN
Washington and Mason Streets, Nob Hill

The cable cars are city landmarks that operate today much the same as they did when Andrew S Hallidie guided the first car down the steep Clay Street in 1873. They were unchanged since that date for just over 100 years, but in 1982 they went under total overhaul and were equipped with new tracks, cables, turntables and winding gear.

The control center for today's fleet has become a museum, in a

The historic cable cars have served the city for almost 120 years

three-tiered, 1907, red-brick barn. From the mezzanine gallery you can see exactly how everything works and also from below deck, from a new glass-enclosed room, you can observe the huge sheaves of cable that guide the cars from under the street. But there is more to be seen here. The building is a storehouse of memorabilia: scale models, photographs and original cars like Hallidie's prototype No 8. To back it up, a 16-minute film, *The Cable Car and How It Works*, is shown continuously. And all this is free.

Open: daily 10:00A.M.–5:00P.M. (until 6:00P.M. May to September). For information call 474-1887.

◆◆◆
CALIFORNIA ACADEMY OF SCIENCES
Golden Gate Park

One roof covers a whole day's worth of enjoyment for there are

many fascinating exhibits that relate to the natural sciences. One of the major attractions is the **Steinhart Aquarium**, which contains a particularly diverse collection of marine life. It includes the Fish Roundabout, with visitors standing in the middle of an enormous circular aquarium where fast swimming schools of fish parade by. Dolphins and seals are fed daily every two hours, beginning at 10:30A.M. (except Thursday at 12:30P.M.); penguins at 11:30A.M. and 2:00P.M..

The second big attraction is the **Morrison Planetarium** which presents several different sky shows each year as well as laser shows on certain evenings (call 750-7141) for sky show information and 750-7138 about laser shows).

Within the Academy visitors may learn more about the

Visitors to the Steinhart Aquarium can watch the dolphins being fed

state's wildlife in **Wild California** and also about humans and evolution in **Life Through Time**. The **Wattis Hall of Human Cultures** displays lifelike scenes to portray how people have adapted to the environment, whether it be the icy setting endured by the Arctic Inuit or the parched desert that is home to the Australian Aborigine. There are also halls devoted to gems and minerals, prehistoric fossils, animals and plants and outer space. The "Safe Quake," in the Earth and Space Hall, allows visitors to experience a simulation of a Californian earthquake. Highly recommended for all the family. *Open*: daily 10:00A.M.–5:00P.M. (later in summer). Admission charge (plus extra for Planetarium shows) but free entrance first Wednesday of the month to the museum, and always free for under-sixes. For information call 221-5100.

CALIFORNIA HISTORICAL SOCIETY (see **Whittier Mansion** under **Historic Buildings and Ships**, page 22).

◆◆◆
CALIFORNIA PALACE OF THE LEGION OF HONOR
Lincoln Park
Atop its Lincoln Park hill, the museum, modeled after the Palais de la Légion d'Honneur in Paris, commands a breathtaking view. Given to the city by the Spreckels family in 1924 it has become a showplace for European art from the Middle Ages to our own century. There is special emphasis on the French Masters of the 18th and 19th centuries, among them de la Tour, Boucher, Fragonard, Watteau, Manet, Monet, Renoir, Cézanne and Degas, although these days there are also Spanish, Dutch, Flemish, Italian and German works of art.
The Rodin sculpture collection is outstanding, including one of the 13 casts of *The Thinker* in the inner courtyard, and French decorative arts are just as strongly represented, including a magnificent 18th-century original Parisian salon.
Also represented by masterpieces are Rembrandt, Rubens, Goya, El Greco, Titian, Tintoretto and others, plus a large collection of graphics. In addition to the permanent exhibits temporary showings of prints and drawings are usually on view, and on weekend afternoons, visitors may enjoy free pipe organ concerts.
Open: Wednesday to Sunday 10:00A.M.–5:00P.M.. Admission charge (under-12s free) but free to all first Wednesday in each month and first Saturday before noon. Admission includes entry to the Asian Art Museum and the de Young Museum if visited on the same day. For information call 750-3600.

◆◆
CARTOON ART MUSEUM
665 Third Street (5th floor)
This unusual museum exhibits original cartoon art on a rotating basis. On display is the actual artwork from which cartoons are made, examples of newspaper strips and magazine panels as well as the book and animated form.
Open: Wednesday to Saturday 11:00A.M.–5:00P.M., (from 10:00A.M. Saturday). Admission charge. For information call 546-3922.

◆
CHINESE CULTURE CENTER
750 Kearny Street, on the 3rd floor of the Holiday Inn
This center was established in the 1970s both as a meeting place for the local community and as a museum which displays Chinese arts and culture.
Many of the exhibits, which frequently change, concentrate on contemporary Asian art and the Center's 450-seat theater is used for performing arts programs.
You can book a heritage walk of Chinatown from here on Wednesdays at 10:30A.M. or inquire about culinary tours.
Open: Tuesday to Saturday 10:00A.M.–4:00P.M.. Admission free. For information call 986-1822.

MUSEUMS

◆
CHINESE HISTORICAL SOCIETY OF AMERICA
650 Commercial Street, Chinatown
This free museum shows the part that the Chinese played in California's Gold Rush and in the subsequent rapid development of the West. On display are artifacts, documents and photographs.
Open: Tuesday to Saturday noon–4:00P.M.. For information call 391-1188.

◆◆◆
EXPLORATORIUM
Palace of Fine Arts, 3601 Lyon Street at Marina Boulevard
The Exploratorium occupies a large part of the Palace of Fine Arts. It is a super science museum that has been acclaimed internationally for its 700-odd tested exhibits which may be manipulated, push-button activated and generally "worked" with. A number of these were created in the Exploratorium's own machine shop and electronics lab by members of staff. All exhibits and their use are explained in this Tactile Gallery.
Open: Wednesday 10:00A.M.–9:30P.M.; Thursday to Sunday 10:00A.M.–5:00P.M.. Admission charge (valid for six months, lifetime for seniors), but under-sixes free (and free to all on the first Wednesday of the month and every Wednesday after 6:00P.M.). For information call 563-7337.

◆
FRIENDS OF PHOTOGRAPHY
Ansel Adams Center, 250 Fourth Street
A recently opened specialist museum with five galleries of photography, one especially devoted to photographer Ansel Adams.
Open: Tuesday to Sunday 11:00A.M.–6:00P.M.. Admission charge (under-12s free). For information call 495-7000.

◆
INTERNATIONAL TOY MUSEUM
The Cannery, 2801 Leavenworth, Fisherman's Wharf
Emphasis is on historic toys from around the world, but the play area's new toys also prove fun for all ages.
Open: Tuesday to Saturday 10:30A.M.–5:00P.M., Sunday 11:00A.M.–5:00P.M.. Admission charge but under-twos free. For information call 441-8627.

◆
JEWISH COMMUNITY MUSEUM
121 Steuart Street (Lower Market)
A museum concerned with past and present Jewish art and culture with frequent special exhibits and multimedia presentations.
Open: Tuesday to Friday and Sunday 10:00A.M.–4:00P.M. (closed some national and Jewish holidays). Free except for major exhibitions. For information call 543-8880.

◆
MEXICAN MUSEUM
Building D, Fort Mason, Laguna Street and Marina Boulevard
This unique museum has constantly changing exhibits including items from the pre-Hispanic period to Chicano (Indian-Hispanic) art of the

present day, with examples of the colonial period and folk art. *Open*: Wednesday to Sunday noon–5:00P.M.. Admission charge except for under-10s accompanied by an adult and free to all on the first Wednesday of each month when open until 8:00P.M.. For information call 441-0404.

◆◆◆
M H DE YOUNG MEMORIAL MUSEUM
Golden Gate Park
The city's oldest and largest art museum whose maze of galleries displays an exciting range of treasures from pre-Columbian gold to masterpieces by Rembrandt and Gainsborough. Its diversity has made it one of California's most popular museums, and its collection of American art ranks among the country's finest. The latter spans the time from the colonial period to the mid-20th century. Among the highlights are a triple portrait of *The Mason Children* (1670); portraits by John Singleton

Copley, Charles Willson Peale and Gilbert Stuart; 19th-century scenes of daily life by George Caleb Bingham; and a complementary selection of American furniture and ornaments.
British art is represented by Reynolds, Raeburn and Thomas Lawrence as well as Gainsborough, but the rest of the world is not forgotten as there are examples of arts from the rest of Europe, Oceania, Africa and Egypt, plus oriental rugs from the famous H McCoy Jones Collection. Tours of the museum are available – consult the schedule at the entrance.
Open: Wednesday to Sunday 10:00A.M.–5:00P.M. (until 8.45P.M. on Wednesday). Admission charge, but under-12s free, and free to all on the first Wednesday and first Saturday morning of each month. For information call 750-3600.

The imposing Museum of Modern Art houses an impressive collection of 20th-century art

MUSEUMS

◆◆◆
MUSEUM OF MODERN ART

*Veteran's Memorial Building,
Civic Center, Van Ness Avenue
and McAllister Street*
The best of 20th-century art is
displayed in the many galleries
of this museum on the third and
fourth floors of the Veteran's
Memorial Building. The permanent
collection includes distinguished
works by modern masters such
as Henri Matisse, of the modern
French school, Swiss artist Paul
Klee, and American artists
Alexander Calder and Jackson
Pollock. But the museum is also a
showcase for work by a number
of local painters and sculptors
who still work in the area and is

*The National Maritime Museum,
looking like a stranded ocean liner*

the venue for changing exhibitions
of a wide range of work of national
and international merit.
Open: Tuesday to Friday
10:00A.M.–5:00P.M. (Thursday
evening to 9:00P.M.); weekends
11:00A.M.–5:00P.M.. Admission
charge, except for under-12s
and the first Tuesday of the
month when it is free to all. Half
price on Thursdays after 5:00P.M..
For information call 863-8800.

◆◆◆
NATIONAL MARITIME
MUSEUM

*San Francisco Maritime National
Historical Park, Aquatic Park at the
foot of Polk Street*
San Francisco has always been a
city of sea and ships and this
museum explores its nautical
past. There are scale models and
shipping relics on the first floor
alongside carved and painted
figureheads. More models can
be seen in the Steamship Room,
this time portraying the great
liners, freighters and US navy
vessels that used to make
frequent voyages through the
Golden Gate. The second floor is
designated "Old Waterfront,"
and again features models and
relics, plus maps, photographs,
paintings and nautical
handicrafts.
Open: daily 10:00A.M.–5:00P.M.
(extended hours in summer).
The museum is free, but there is
a charge for Hyde Street Pier
(see page 20), except under-17s
and seniors who go free. For
information call 556-8177.

◆
PACIFIC HERITAGE MUSEUM

*Bank of Canton Building, 608
Commercial Street at
Montgomery Street*

Free for all who want to view changing displays of the history of the artistic, cultural, economic and other interchanges between those peoples on both sides of the Pacific Basin. A permanent exhibit documents the history of the first US Branch Mint and subtreasury buildings.
Open: weekdays 10:00A.M.–4:00P.M..
Call 399-1124 for weekend times.

PRESIDIO ARMY MUSEUM
Lincoln Boulevard and Funston Avenue, Building 2 Presidio
One of the Presidio's (see page 30) oldest buildings, dating to the 1860s when it was the Old Station Hospital, has been converted into a military museum showing the role the military played in the history and development of the city from 1776 to the present. Two restored "earthquake" cottages stand on the grounds, having been moved from their original sites.
Open: daily except Monday 10:00A.M.–4:00P.M. Guided tours are available by reservation (call 921-8193). Admission free.
For information call 561-4115.

SAN FRANCISCO AFRICAN-AMERICAN HISTORICAL AND CULTURAL SOCIETY
Building C, Fort Mason Center, entrance at Marina Boulevard and Laguna Street
This museum contains exhibits relating to the history of blacks in California and African art collections.
Open: Wednesday to Sunday

noon–5:00P.M.. Donation welcome. For information call 441-0640.

SAN FRANCISCO CRAFT AND FOLK ART MUSEUM
Landmark Building A, Fort Mason Center
The museum displays contemporary arts and crafts from around the world.
Open: Tuesday to Sunday 11:00A.M.–5:00P.M. (Saturday from 10:00A.M.). Admission charge but children under 12 free. Also free every Saturday morning. For information call 775-0990.

SAN FRANCISCO FIRE DEPARTMENT PIONEER MEMORIAL MUSEUM
655 Presidio Avenue at Pine Street
Specialized museum devoted to the various fire companies, most especially those volunteer units which existed between 1849 and 1866. There is also a large exhibit concentrating on the famous fire buff, Lillie Hitchcock Coit. The most historic items here are the fire trumpets, hand pumpers and the city's first ever fire engine.
Open: weekends only 1:00–4:00P.M. (guided tours available). Free entry.
For information call 861-8000 ext 365.

SAN FRANCISCO HISTORY ROOM AND ARCHIVES
Public Library (third floor), Larkin and McAllister Streets
A history museum in miniature where exhibits often change. The maps, photographs,

newspapers, documents and artifacts (old and new) are of undeniable interest. The History Room is part of the Civic Center complex (see pages 22–4).
Open: Thursday and Saturday 10:00A.M.–6:00P.M., Tuesday and Friday noon–6:00P.M. and Wednesday 1:00–6:00P.M.. Free entry. For information call 558-3949.

◆
SOCIETY OF CALIFORNIA PIONEERS
Pioneer Hall, 456 McAllister Street
The Society maintains a museum of 19th-century Californian art and the Children's History Gallery with items from the Gold Rush.
Open: Monday to Friday 10:00A.M.–4:00P.M.; closed August. Admission free. For information call 861-5278.

◆
TREASURE ISLAND MUSEUM
Building One to the right of the Treasure Island main gate
Treasure Island was the site of the 1939 Golden Gate International Exposition. Historic highlights of the three Pacific sea services – Navy, Marine Corps and Coast Guard – are to be seen in the Pacific Panorama Gallery. Here exhibits include "Sovereigns of the Sea," which tells the story of the US's battleships, one dedicated to the China Clipper flying boats of the 1930s, and one which recalls the 1939 Exposition.
Open: daily in summer 10:00A.M.–3:30P.M.; closed during winter. Free entry. For information call 395-5067.

WAX MUSEUM
145 Jefferson Street, Fisherman's Wharf
Four floors of life-sized and authentically dressed wax figures. Highlights include the Hall of Religions, Palace of Living Art, Chamber of Horrors, Gallery of Stars and Tutankhamun's Tomb.
Open: daily 9:00A.M.–10:00P.M. (Friday and Saturday in summer until midnight). Admission charge but under-sixes free. For information call 885-4975.

◆
WELLS FARGO HISTORY MUSEUM
Wells Fargo Bank, 420 Montgomery Street
The best of the West, from the time of Wells Fargo's founding in the Gold Rush era to the early 1900s. An intriguing assortment of photographs, gold nuggets, miners' equipment and guns in a room of the bank's headquarters, all dominated by a Concord stagecoach.
Open: Monday to Friday 9:00A.M.–5:00P.M.. Free entry. For information call 396-2619.

Outdoor Attractions

ALCATRAZ ISLAND
San Francisco Bay
It is only 1½ miles (2.5km) from the shores of San Francisco but Alcatraz used to send shivers down many a convict's spine, because for many years it was a federal prison that housed such notorious criminals as Al Capone and Robert Stroud, known as the "Birdman of

Alcatraz Island once housed some of this country's most notorious criminals

Alcatraz.'' It saw its first prisoners during the Civil War but it was only later that "The Rock," as it was nicknamed, became so feared.

It was named by the Spaniards who, when they spotted the island, saw it was covered with pelicans and therefore called it "Isla de los Alcatraces." The island was the site chosen for the first lighthouse on the Pacific coast (in 1854) and it was only afterwards that the fortifications were gradually added.

Today, as part of the Golden Gate National Recreation Area, it is tranquil again, a must for the visitor's itinerary, though you, too, might shiver as you gaze at the windswept prison yard with its wall-topped guard towers. The National Park Service these days conducts tours through the main cell block though there are audio-cassette tours if you plan to take the self-guided trail. For information call 556-0560 (weekdays 9:30A.M.–4:30P.M.). Red and White Fleet boats leave frequently for the island from Fisherman's Wharf, Pier 41 (call 546-2896 for boat information; 546-2882 for advance ticket purchases). It is advisable to buy tickets in advance, especially in the high season, though tickets are obtainable on the day from Pier 41 on a first-come-first served basis.

◆
ANGEL ISLAND STATE PARK
San Francisco Bay
This is the largest island in the Bay, first discovered by the

Spanish who gave it its name "Señora de los Angeles" before a Los Angeles ever existed. Over the years it has been a dueling ground, a staging area for soldiers and a quarantine station. Today it is a 740-acre (300-hectare) preserve.

Relics of the past are found in a small museum and a partially restored immigration station. There are three trails trisecting the island, a retreat for bicyclists, hikers and picnickers alike, plus camping facilities. Call 435-1915 for park information.

It is easily reached by using the Angel Island State Park ferry from Tiburon (call 435-2131 for schedules) or the Red and White Fleet's ferry service which, during the summer, operates daily from Fisherman's Wharf, Pier 43½ (call 546-2815 for details) and Vallejo to Ayala Cove on the island, named after the 18th-century Spanish discoverer, Juan Manuel de Ayala.

◆

AQUATIC PARK
foot of Polk Street
A popular bayside municipal park three blocks west of Fisherman's Wharf that encompasses a small beach and the National Maritime Museum (see page 36). Local fishermen are often to be seen casting a line from the pier here.

◆

CHINA BEACH
28th Avenue and Sea Cliff between Lincoln Park and the Presidio
A 600-foot (180m) long sandy beach that is often used for sunbathing and picnicking. Facilities include sun decks and changing rooms. The name stems from the time when the Chinese fishermen used to camp here. It is easily reached on the 38 or 38L bus departing from Geary westbound to 25th Avenue and then via a transfer to northbound 29. Exit at El Camino del Mar and walk four blocks west.

◆◆

GOLDEN GATE NATIONAL RECREATION AREA
This vast protected area was created in 1972 to provide an urban park for the densely

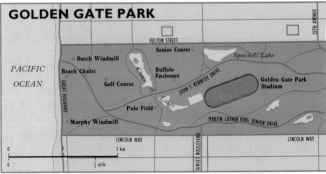

Memorial to Cervantes, one of many unusual sights in Golden Gate Park

populated city. It embraces islands, maritime parks, yacht harbors, ocean beaches, obsolete military posts and historic points of interest as well as the undeveloped Marin headlands across the Golden Gate Bridge with wildlife sanctuaries, picnic sites and miles of trails. Information on activities can be obtained from the park headquarters at Fort Mason (see page 25).

♦♦♦
GOLDEN GATE PARK
from Stanyan Street to the Ocean, between Fulton Street and Lincoln Way
Much of the taming of what were barren sand dunes was the work of Scottish landscape gardener, John McLaren, Park Superintendent from 1887 to 1943. Development has been continuous since 1871 so that this fine park, extending three miles (5km) from the middle of the peninsula to the ocean shore, today offers tracts of green lawns, bridle-paths, foot trails, lakes and flowers, as well as being the beautiful setting for several museums.

To the north of the main J F Kennedy Drive you will find the

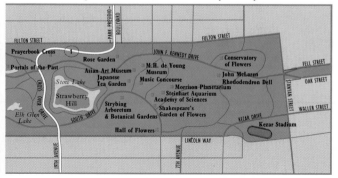

Conservatory of Flowers (see page 25), modeled after the great greenhouse in Kew Gardens in England. To the south of the main drive is the **John McLaren Rhododendron Dell**, named for the man affectionately known as Uncle John. On a warm Sunday, band concerts are given outdoors in the tree-sheltered **Music Concourse** which was created for an 1894 exhibition, as was the **Japanese Tea Garden**, an oriental garden with miniature trees, mini-waterfalls, Shinto shrines and a wishing bridge. It is at its best at cherry blossom time. *Garden open:* daily 9:00A.M.–6:30P.M. (8:30A.M.–5:30P.M. October to February). Tea served in the teahouse 10:30A.M.–5:30P.M.. Admission charge except for under-sixes and on the first Wednesday of each month.

Flanking the concourse is the **California Academy of Sciences** (see page 31-2) and, across the way, the **Asian Art Museum** and **M H de Young Memorial Museum** (see pages 30 and 35). Also nearby is **Shakespeare's Garden of Flowers**, where every tree, plant and flower ever mentioned in a work by the bard can be found. On South Drive, **Strybing Arboretum and Botanical Gardens** are a highlight for those interested in botany. Many of the 6,000 plants growing here are unique, and those native to

The Conservatory of Flowers was shipped from England in the 1870s

California have their own section.

In the Gardens of Fragrance, even the vision impaired benefit, as all the plants here are pleasant to smell and to touch and are labeled in Braille. *Gardens open:* 8:00A.M.–4:30P.M. Monday to Friday, 10:00A.M.–5:00P.M. weekends and holidays, with guided tours at 1:30P.M., and also at 10:30A.M. weekends. Admission free. Off South Drive you will find **Stow Lake**, not only the central reservoir but a popular boating spot. Use the stepping stones across the lake to **Strawberry Hill**, the park's highest point, where a spiraling path takes you to a gorgeous viewing point. Explorers in the western section of the park will discover the Chain of Lakes, Dutch windmills, a polo field and Spreckels Lake used by model boat enthusiasts. Just off Kennedy Drive, there is even a small herd of buffalo. A favorite with children, a 1912-vintage Hershel-Spillman restored merry-go-round is in the playground.

Free guided tours of selected parts of the park are offered on weekends from May to October (call 221-1311).

Best way to reach the park is via a westbound 5 bus (Fulton) or a 21 (Hayes) on Market Street, both routed along the north side of the park. Then transfer to a southbound 44 at Eighth Avenue or walk south into the park. For information call 666-7200.

◆
LAKE MERCED
What was an ocean lagoon has become a popular water playground for San Franciscans and is now fed by freshwater springs. Good for boating and trout fishing, this large lake lies adjacent to the zoo in the southwest corner of the city. It is best reached by the M Muni-Metro line to 19th Avenue and Winston Drive and then a transfer to a southbound 18 bus on 19th Avenue.

◆
LINCOLN PARK
west of Presidio, main entrance at Clement Street and 34th Avenue
A 270-acre (110-hectare) green area on the headlands of Point Lobos providing dramatic vistas of the Golden Gate from the 200-foot (60m) cliffs. Principal park attractions are the **California Palace of the Legion of Honor** (see page 33) and the municipal golf course.

◆
MARINA GREEN
bayshore from Webster Street to Scott Street
A broad belt of lawn by the waterfront, this is a good place for the energetic to work out and for sightseers and boat enthusiasts it is a first-class viewing area of San Francisco's yacht harbor and any weekend regattas.

◆
MEDIEVAL DUNGEON
Wax Museum Entertainment Complex, 145 Jefferson Street
Fourteenth-century life has been recreated electronically in this interesting and unusual museum. A clear impression of the prisons in those times can be experienced.
Open: 9:00A.M.–11:30P.M. (Friday and Saturday until midnight).

Under-sixes free. For further information call 885-4975.

OCEAN BEACH

western edge of the city, along Great Highway

An area of surf and sand, linking Fort Funston with Cliff House, with Seal Rocks the major attraction. These are small stony islands offshore at the foot of Point Lobos Avenue and inhabited by sea lions from September to June. From downtown, take any 5, 31 or 38 bus marked Ocean Beach (westbound).

SEAL ROCKS

foot of Point Lobos Avenue

Lovers of nature and birdlife should head for these offshore outcrops usually inhabited by shore birds and sea lions (September–June). Bring binoculars for better viewing. On clear days the Farallone Islands are visible even though they are 30 miles (48km) away.

SIGMUND STERN GROVE

19th Avenue and Sloat Boulevard

This pleasant historic glen, sheltered from the hot afternoon sun by redwood and fir trees, forms a natural amphitheater adjacent to Pine Lake Park and is a good area for a family outing. It is the setting on summer Sunday afternoons for outdoor concerts, opera and ballet performances.

There are also facilities for family picnics, lawn bowling, croquet and putting.

TWIN PEAKS

There are wonderful views of the whole of the beautiful Bay area from this 65-acre (26-hectare) park in the center of the city, reached via Twin Peaks Boulevard. Take along your camera for some memorable viewing. In the old days the crests were referred to as "Los Pechos de la Chola" (the breasts of the Indian girl).

Something Different

ACRES OF ORCHIDS

1450 El Camino Real, south San Francisco, in the airport area, 8 miles (13km) from town

Just 20 minutes from downtown (take Hickey Boulevard exit east from Interstate 280 to El Camino – State Route 82) is this spectacular nursery, where greenhouse after greenhouse is lined up.

The free tour covers an incomparable collection of thousands of orchids in a lush and beautiful tropical garden which is also a showcase for other unusual plants. Avid gardeners should not miss the viewing of orchid cloning in the laboratories. There is also a range of gift items on sale.

Open: 8:00A.M.–5:00P.M. with tours at 10:30A.M. and 1:30P.M.. For information call 871-5655.

CHEVRON, A WORLD OF OIL

555 Market Street (lobby level)

A free exhibit which tells the story of oil, from the way it is found to how it is brought up

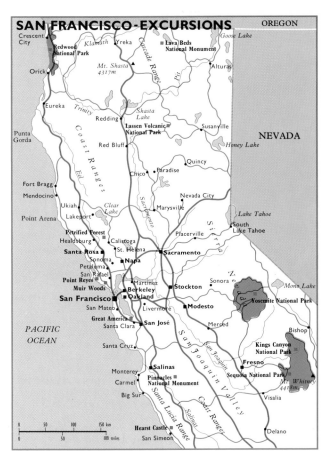

SAN FRANCISCO-EXCURSIONS

OREGON

Crescent City · Klamath · Yreka · Lava Beds National Monument · Goose Lake

Redwood National Park

Orick · Mt. Shasta 4317m · Alturas

Eureka · Trinity · Shasta Lake · Pit · Redding · Susanville · NEVADA

Punta Gorda · Lassen Volcanic National Park · Honey Lake

Red Bluff

Fort Bragg · Chico · Paradise · Quincy

Mendocino · Nevada City

Ukiah · Clear Lake · Marysville · Lake Tahoe

Point Arena · Lakeport · South Lake Tahoe

Petrified Forest · Placerville

Healdsburg · Calistoga

Santa Rosa · St. Helena · Sacramento

Sonoma · Napa

Petaluma · Sonora · Mono Lake

San Rafael

Point Reyes · Martinez · Stockton

Muir Woods · Berkeley

San Francisco · Oakland · Modesto · Yosemite National Park

San Mateo · Livermore

Great America · Merced · Bishop

PACIFIC OCEAN · Santa Clara · San José

Santa Cruz · Kings Canyon National Park

Monterey · Salinas · Fresno

Carmel · Pinnacles National Monument · Sequoia National Park · Mt. Whitney 4418m

Big Sur · Visalia

Hearst Castle · Delano

San Simeon

Coast Ranges · Eel · Sacramento · Sierra Nevada · San Joaquin Valley · Santa Lucia Range · Salinas · Coast Ranges · Cascade Range

from underground, and how it is transformed into the finished products it becomes part of. The story is explained and made interesting by way of moving displays, working models and oil field equipment. Visitors may request to see an audiovisual presentation.
Open: Monday to Friday 9:00A.M.–4:00P.M.. For information call 894-5193.

◆

HAUNTED GOLD MINE

Wax Museum Entertainment Complex, 145 Jefferson Street
Fun for the family, featuring a fascinating array of illusions and fantasy with a forty-niners' theme.
Open: daily 9:00A.M.–11:00P.M. (except Friday and Saturday until midnight in summer). Admission charge.

EXCURSIONS

Getting Out and About

Stand at the top of any of San Francisco's seven principal hills and the view of the great outdoors is incomparable. The city is, after all, surrounded by parkland and water. The rim of the city – the waterfront promenade, Aquatic Park, the Golden Gate Promenade winding its way through Fort Mason and Marina Green to Crissy Field, a shoreline retreat next to the Presidio – is an oceanside walk. At Ocean Beach, the city's westernmost edge, there is a four-mile (6.5km) sandy shoreline pounded by Pacific rollers. On the city's northern edge, China Beach is one of the few city beaches where swimming is safe (watched by lifeguards in summer). Visit Baker Beach for the views only as swimming here is dangerous. For information on other city open areas see **Outdoor Attractions**, pages 38-44.

Beyond the city there is plenty of open space and it is easily reached. Marin County is looked upon as the "Mediterranean" side of the bay, where **Sausalito** ("Little Willow"), likened to Portofino in Italy, has picturesque houses cascading down the slopes to a waterfront thick with yachts and houseboats. It is only eight miles (13km) north of the city and accessible via road or ferry service. So is **Tiburon** (16 miles/26km from the city), a colorful harbor town on Raccoon Strait where several restaurants have bayside service. The same distance north of the skyscrapers is much loved **Muir Woods**, a cool and shady retreat in summer for a walk or picnic beneath the towering sequoia.

East of the city, along the mainland side of the Bay, is **Oakland** (eight miles/13km), whose estuary is embellished by Jack London Square, and **Berkeley** (12miles/19km), an oak-shaded campus of the University of California.

The peninsula to the south flanking the Pacific is indented by coves popular with surfers, and **Santa Cruz**, a two-hour drive, has acres of lifeguarded beaches. In the forested environs of Santa Cruz are two peaceful state redwood preserves, the **Henry W Cowell Park** and **Big Basin**, as well as two restored excursion railways, the **Roaring Camp and Big Trees Narrow-Gauge Railroad** at Felton and the **Big Trees and Pacific** between Santa Cruz and Olympia. Farther south is the lovely seaside resort of **Carmel** with its sandy beaches, cozy inns and chic boutiques and craft galleries. Together with the historic town **Monterey**, it is one of the most scenic spots on the California coast.

Many areas of interest to nature-lovers are described in the **Peace and Quiet** section (see page 62). In addition, a longer trip can be made to **Redwood National Park**, 330 miles (530km) north of San Francisco on US 101. The park comprises 106,000 acres (43,000 hectares), partly in Humboldt county and partly in Del Norte and, as its name suggests, it is full of giant redwood trees.

Within the designated area are three state parks: **Del Norte Coast Redwoods State Park**, off

Highway 101, near Crescent City (call (707) 464-9533 for information Monday to Friday 8:00A.M.–5:00P.M.); **Jedediah Smith Redwoods State Park**, off Highway 199, east of Crescent City (call (707) 458-3310); and **Prairie Creek Redwoods State Park**, off Highway 101, just north of Orick (call (707) 488-2171).

◆
BERKELEY
East Bay
This is the headquarters of the University of California campus whose students are historically known for their radical politics. From the campus site and also from Berkeley's marina, there are countless photogenic views of the Bay and Golden Gate Bridge. You can take a tour of the campus which boasts an excellent Hall of Science, Art Museum, Museum of

Anthropology and Botanical Garden.

◆◆◆
BIG SUR
32 miles (51km) south of Monterey Peninsula
Not to be done in a day, but this celebrated portion of scenic coastline has such a rare beauty that almost everyone wants to pass this way. The surf pounds the shore below and the Santa Lucia mountain range rises above. City-dwellers come here for weekend getaways. A focal point of the area is the **Pfeiffer Big Sur State Park** where hiking trails lead into redwood groves and rustic cabins or rooms at the Big Sur Lodge (call (408) 667-2171) may be rented.

The Big Sur coast, a good place to get away from the fumes of the city

EXCURSIONS

Hikers, skiers and gamblers can all enjoy a trip to beautiful Lake Tahoe

LAKE TAHOE
200 miles (320km) east of San Francisco
Lake Tahoe, 22 miles (35km) long and 12 miles (19km) wide, offers a wide range of facilities to suit different people. It is a natural pure lake, so clear that you can see the rocky bottom at an astonishing depth on a glass-bottomed boat tour.

Ringed by craggy mountains, the lake is both a summer and winter resort. The wealthy élite choose the gentler slopes on the north shore; the mass of visitors heads for the more active south shore. In winter, the key ski resorts are Squaw Valley and Heavenly Valley. Throughout the year Lake Tahoe's casinos work overtime, especially at the state border (with Nevada). A visitor

center, situated on State Route 89 between Camp Richardson and Emerald Bay, provides guided walks daily in summer (call (916) 573-2600).

MARTINEZ
East Bay
John Muir, the conservationist, prominent in the establishment of the US national parks and forests, once lived here and, although it is no longer the pastoral center he knew, you can visit the **John Muir National Historic Site**, 4202 Alhambra Avenue (call (415) 228-8860), a restored 17-room Victorian house built in 1882 and surrounded by orchards and vineyards. Also on the site is the **Martinez Adobe**, built in 1849. *Site open*: 10:00A.M.–4:30P.M.

(summer). Admission charge, but under-16s and seniors free.

◆◆◆
MENDOCINO COAST
180 miles (290km) north of San Francisco
The quaint preserved Victorian town of Mendocino was built by New Englanders for lumber, and its white church spires, weathered wooden houses and position on a seashore bluff give it the look of many a real New England town. Actually, it is little more than a village and its picturesque qualities attracted numerous artists to the area when the timber business declined. The **Kelly House Historical Museum**, at 45007 Albion Street, explains the histories of private buildings in the area, North of San Francisco along this coastal route is delightful for touring (for information call (707) 937-5791).

◆◆◆
MONTEREY PENINSULA
94 miles (151km) south of San Francisco
Monterey was so named to honor the Spanish Count Mont-Ray who was viceroy of Mexico in 1602, but it was Father Junípero Serra's missionary party who rediscovered it and founded the *presidio* here and the Mission San Carlos de Borromeo at Carmel. For a long time, Monterey was a whalers' retreat, but once the fishing industry had expanded, the town became a terminus for the anchovy and sardine fleets. The peninsula's three tourist centers are Monterey, Carmel and

Pacific Grove in a setting of such beautiful seascapes and superlative golf courses that the whole area is in a class of its own. What had become economically obsolete in Monterey (the fish canneries) have become pure tourist attractions, while Carmel has developed arts and crafts and its inn and restaurant business without expanding its size (the center of town is a six-block square). Prim little Pacific Grove is mainly residential because development was not allowed until the 1970s.
One of the best ways to view it all is to take the **17-Mile Drive**, a toll road which loops its way around the peninsula's shoreline, passing handsome rocky headlands like Cypress Point, super golf courses such as Pebble Beach and Spy Glass Hill and splendid homes built between the two World Wars. There are three gates to the Drive – at Monterey, at Carmel Hill and at Carmel.
Attractions in **Monterey** include the **Allen Knight Maritime Museum**, 550 Calle Principal, Monterey, which houses a large maritime collection including the old Fresnel Light (1880) from Point Sur Lighthouse and a scale model of the *Savannah*, Commodore John Drake Sloat's flagship when he took possession of Monterey in 1846 and declared California part of the United States.
Open: Tuesday to Friday 10:00A.M.–4:00P.M.; weekends 2:00–4:00P.M. (mid-June to mid-September); Tuesday to Friday 1:00–4:00P.M. rest of year. Admission free.

EXCURSIONS

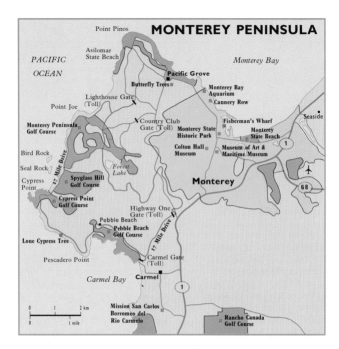

For information call (408) 375-2553.

Cannery Row is the big must. The name goes back to those times when fishermen might haul in 240,000 tons of sardines, which inspired John Steinbeck's book *Cannery Row*. Today this restored area features fine restaurants, shops and galleries.

Monterey Bay Aquarium at No 886 Cannery Row is the largest aquarium in the US. Here 6,5000 creatures fill 100 habitat galleries and exhibits, and the visitor experiences the illusion of being at the bottom of the ocean with the underwater life in Monterey Bay, including sharks and sea otters.

Aquarium open: daily 9:30A.M.–6:00P.M. (from 10:00A.M. in winter). Admission charge. Call (408) 648-4800 for information. Changing exhibits on Monterey's history may be seen at the **Colton Hall Museum**, on Pacific Street, which was the site of California's first constitutional convention in 1849. Adjoining the hall is the old jail built in 1854.

Open: daily 10:00A.M.–5:00P.M. (closing at 4:00P.M. Monday to Friday in winter). Free.

From **Fisherman's Wharf** in Monterey you can take a whale-watching cruise (December to March) or fishing trip and feed the sea lions and otters.

American art is emphasized at the **Monterey Peninsula Museum of Art**, 559 Pacific Street, along with photography and graphics, Asian art and international folk art.
Open: Tuesday to Saturday 10:00A.M.–4:00P.M., Sunday 1:00–4:00P.M.. Donations. For information call (408) 372-7591.

Monterey State Historic Park, at 20 Custom House Plaza, comprises eight 19th-century buildings: the Custom House (the state's oldest government building, 1827); Pacific House (1847, housing a collection of American Indian artifacts); First Theater (the state's first, built as an adobe boarding house/saloon); Casa del Oro (a restored general store exhibiting early trade items); Casa Soberanes' Larkin House (home in the 1840s to Thomas Larkin, first US consul to Mexico in Monterey); Stevenson House (where the Scottish writer Robert Louis Stevenson spent three months in 1879); and Cooper-Molera Adobe (the restored Victorian home of a Yankee sea captain). These buildings are staffed all year for guided tours, but opening times for individual sites vary – call (408) 649-2836 for information.

"Oldtown" Salinas is a busy little place that was once the writer John Steinbeck's home. **Steinbeck House**, at 132 Central Avenue (call (408) 424-2735), was his birthplace and now operates as a restaurant and gift shop. Steinbeck memorabilia are displayed in the John Steinbeck Public Library at 110 West San Luis Street.

More of the area's history is displayed at **José Eusibio Boronda Adobe**, a museum and one of the oldest existing adobes (buildings of sun-dried brick), located at the northwest edge of Salinas half a mile (1km) from Highway 101 at 333 Boronda Road.
Open: Monday to Friday 9:00A.M.–3:00P.M., Sunday 1:00–4:00P.M., with tours Saturday by appointment.

The **Harvey-Baker House** (1868), the oldest house in Salinas, is near the Memorial Hospital.
Open: Sundays 1:00–4:00P.M..

Apart from being a delightful place to stay, eat and shop, **Carmel** is known for its **Mission San Carlos Borromeo del Rio Carmelo**, 3080 Rio Road, in whose basilica Father Junípero Serra is buried. Its graceful proportions and fine detailing made it one of the finest of the 21 missions and it is now restored to near perfect condition.
Open: Monday to Saturday 9:30A.M.–4:30P.M., Sunday 10:30A.M.–4:30P.M.. Donations accepted. For information call (408) 624-3600.

At Carmel Point, **Tor House** was built for Robinson Jeffers, one of the West's important poets in the early 1900s. Stones from Carmel Beach were used for its construction and that of **Hawk Tower**, a retreat built on the grounds. All Jeffers' major works were written here.
Tours are given on Fridays and Saturdays from 10:00A.M. to 3:00P.M. (by reservation only). Admission charge. No under-12s.

EXCURSIONS

For information call (408) 824-1813.

Nature-lovers might note that there are a number of state beaches and that **Point Lobos State Reserve** is situated four miles (6.5km) south of Carmel.

◆◆◆
MOUNT TAMALPAIS STATE PARK
Marin County

This is picturesque coastal hill country dominated by the triple-peaked Mount Tamalpais. Bay area hikers find it a first-class spot, enjoying the grassy meadows and the shade of redwoods. The 6,218-acre (2,516-hectare) park surrounds the **Muir Woods National Monument** and there are hiking possibilities well beyond its borders. Park headquarters are on the Panoramic Highway.

NAPA VALLEY
76 miles (122km) north of San Francisco

The perfect destination for any visitor with a car, this beautiful valley is most noted for its plethora of vineyards. By 1881 they had covered almost as much of the area as they do now and by 1890 the wines being produced had fans in Europe as well as the US. There is a great deal of rural charm in the Napa Valley with its country stores, small towns and country inns, though it does get busy. In addition to wine sampling, visitors come to this region for sports like hot air ballooning and for the health spas at the hot springs.

One of the main towns is

Vineyard in the Napa Valley. Many wineries welcome visitors

Calistoga in the shadow of Mount St Helena at the northern end of the valley, favored for its old-fashioned ambience and its mineral springs and hot mineralized mud baths.

Just to the north, people come to watch **Old Faithful Geyser of California** (Tubbs Lane) erupt on the average of every 40 minutes. This is only one of three of its type in existence.

Open: daily 9:00A.M.–6:00P.M. (to 5:00P.M. in winter). Admission charge but under-sixes free. For information call (707) 942-6463.

Historic materials dating from 1860–1915 are displayed in the city's **Sharpsteen Museum**, 1311 Washington Street.

Open: daily 10:00A.M.–4:00P.M. (from noon November to March).

For information call (707) 942-5911.

On Petrified Forest Road (five miles/8km west) you will find the **Petrified Forest**, the result of Mount St Helena's volcanic eruptions millions of years ago, when a redwood forest was uprooted and covered with ash and infiltrated with silicas and minerals causing the petrification. The grounds contain a museum and picnic facilities.

Open: daily 9:00A.M.–5.45P.M. (to 5:00P.M. in winter). Admission charge but under-10s free.

Seven miles (11km) north of Calistoga, **Robert Louis Stevenson State Park** is where the Scottish writer lived and worked in 1880.

Napa is the largest, most southerly township in the valley. From here the **Napa Valley**

Wine Train, whose depot is at 1275 McKinstry Street, operates to Yountville, Oakville, Rutherford and St Helena. You travel aboard a restored vintage turn-of-the-century train in Pullman cars, and if you take the dinner train you will be served by suitably attired stewards a four-course gourmet spread. Call (707) 253-2111 for more information.

St Helena is another popular stop. The **Silverado Museum** at 1490 Library Lane contains Robert Louis Stevenson memorabilia, including first editions, original manuscripts and photographs.

Open: Tuesday to Sunday noon–4:00P.M.. Free.

For information call (707) 963-3757.

Just to the north is the **Bale Grist Mill State Historic Park**, whose water-powered grist mill was built in 1846.

Open: daily 10:00A.M.–5:00P.M..

For information call (707) 963-2236.

(For locations of Napa Valley wineries see map page 58; a selection of wineries to visit is given on page 81.)

◆
OAKLAND

East Bay

Tourism does not come first for Oakland, which is primarily an industrial city sandwiched between San Francisco and Berkeley. However, if you have money to splurge you may want to take the 194-foot (59m) *Slice Blimp*, an airship that takes off from the north terminal of the airport for one-hour flights over San Francisco Bay all year. Call

EXCURSIONS

568-4101 for more information. In the heart of Oakland is **Lake Merritt**, a very large saltwater tidal lake where the public can sail, canoe, row, take a trip on a miniature sternwheeler or jog the lakeside path. In **Lakeside Park** on the eastern shore is a wildfowl refuge and Children's Fairyland. Another place to take the kids is the **Oakland Zoo** at Knowland Park, 98th Avenue, which gives free weekend elephant shows and does not charge in the petting zoo section. Rides include a miniature railway, merry-go-round and skyride.
Zoo open: 10:00A.M.–4:00P.M. (park open dawn to dusk). Admission charge for zoo.
For information call 632-9525. The **Oakland Museum**, 10th and Oak Streets, illustrates Californian history particularly well and for free. Exhibits relating to natural and human history are seen on the two lower levels and on the top level there is a chronology of Californian art.
Open: Wednesday to Saturday 10:00A.M.–5:00P.M., Sunday noon–7:00P.M..
For information call 273-3401. The city's waterfront and marina area at the foot of Broadway is also an interesting place to be. Here you will find good restaurants, Heinold's First and Last Chance Saloon, Jack London's Yukon Cabin and The Village, a themed shopping complex.
A last suggestion for the architecturally minded is a visit to **Dunsmuir House and Gardens**, 2960 Peralta Oaks Court, a 37-room Colonial Revival-style mansion.
Open: Wednesday and Sunday from April to September for tours at 11:30A.M., 12:30 and 1:30P.M..

SAN MATEO
San Francisco Peninsula
San Mateo is the location of Bay Meadows Race Course and Candlestick Point State Recreation Area and is quite easy to reach from the city. Visit the **Coyote Point Museum**, Coyote Point Drive, where exhibits detail the ecological zones of the Bay area and where computer "games" explain what has to be done in nature, for example, to assemble the ingredients for a hamburger. There are also dioramas and films. A wildlife center houses creatures native to the area, and there are picnic facilities with good views of the Bay area.
Open: Wednesday to Friday 10:00A.M.–5:00P.M., weekends 1:00–5:00P.M.. Admission charge but free on Fridays and for under-sixes. For information call 342-7755.
The story of San Mateo County is told in the **San Mateo County Historical Museum**, 1700 West Hillsdale Boulevard via exhibits, dioramas and models.
Open: Monday to Thursday 9:30A.M.–4:30P.M., Sunday 12:30–4:30P.M.. Donations welcome. For information call 574-6441.

SAN RAFAEL
Marin County
This is one of Marin's four major towns, where the **Mission San**

Rafael Arcangel, founded in
1817 as the 20th in the
Franciscan chain, has been
reconstructed. It is located at
1102 5th Avenue at A Street, (call
454-8141).
Open: daily 11:00A.M.–4:00P.M..
Admission free.
Architecture buffs may care to
take a look also at one of Frank
Lloyd Wright's last great public
buildings – the **Marin County
Civic Center** on the northern
side of town.
If you are an animal lover you
may like to visit the **Wildlife
Center** at 76 Albert Park, a
sanctuary for injured animals.

◆◆◆
SAN SIMEON
*midway between San Francisco
and Los Angeles*
It is still known as Hearst Castle,

*Luxury in the Hollywood style: Roman
swimming pool at Hearst Castle*

although its official name is now
**Hearst-San Simeon State
Historical Monument**. San
Simeon was built in the 1920s for
publishing tycoon William
Randolph Hearst to entertain the
multitude of Hollywood stars and
other celebrities he knew.
Furnishings and ornamentation
were gathered from around the
world, making the end result
the ultimate in Californian
fantasy, an eclectic mix of
Roman, Gothic and other styles.
After Hearst's death, his family
gave the "castle" to the state as a
historic monument. There are
123 acres (50 hectares) of pools,
gardens, terraces and guest
houses (each practically a stately
home in its own right) as well as

EXCURSIONS

the main building. Together they house one of the world's largest and finest private art collections.

You have a choice of three two-hour tours available all through the year. Tickets, which should be reserved in advance, may be purchased at any Mistix outlet or by calling (800) 444-7275. They all involve a certain amount of walking and climbing, and a fourth tour, the Garden Tour, may only be taken from April to October (under-sixes free).

Estate open (for tours only): 9:00A.M.–5:00P.M. in summer; 8.20A.M.–3.20P.M. in winter.

◆◆◆
SANTA CLARA VALLEY
46 miles (74km) south of San Francisco

Irreverently nicknamed the "Silicon Valley," its population seems ever on the increase. **Santa Clara** itself is the location of the **Great America** theme park (see **Children,** page 103). Also here is the **Mission Santa Clara de Asis**, eighth in the string of Missions, founded in 1777 and now part of the Santa Clara University.

The present building is a replica of the mission built in 1826, but the original garden survives.

Open: daily 7:00A.M.–7:00P.M. (museum daily except Monday 11:00A.M.–4:00P.M.). Self-guided tours. Free.

The **Triton Museum**, 1505 Warburton Avenue, which opened in 1987, is worth a visit. Soft natural light allows for better viewing of major national and international exhibitions. The permanent collection here focuses on 19th- and 20th-century American art. The sculpture garden in the grounds can be viewed via the museum's rear glass wall.

Open: Monday to Friday 10:00A.M.–5:00P.M. (Tuesday until 9:00P.M.), weekends noon-5:00P.M.. Free. For information call (408) 247-3754.

Undeclared Valley capital is **San José**, which features a number of attractions for vacationers. Garden buffs will appreciate the **Municipal Rose Garden**, Naglee Avenue between Dana Avenue and Garden Drive, where 7,000 plantings of roses are in bloom in May and June.

Open: daily 8:00A.M. to one-half hour before sunset. For information call (408) 277-4661. At the corner of Naglee Avenue and Park is the **Rosicrucian Egyptian Museum and Planetarium**. One of the West Coast's best collections of Egyptian, Babylonian and Assyrian artifacts is contained in this museum. Highlights include a reproduction of the pharaoh Tutankhamun's sarcophagus and an impressive array of mummies. A wide range of presentations is given in the planetarium.

Open: Tuesday to Sunday 9:00A.M.–5:00P.M.. Admission charge (under-sevens free). No under-fives in the Planetarium. For information call (408) 287-9171.

San José Museum of Art, 110 South Market Street, permanently shows the work of Bay area artists and nationally known names.

Open: Tuesday to Friday 10:00A.M.–6:00P.M., Saturday 10:00A.M.–4:00P.M., Sunday noon–4:00P.M., (guided tours Tuesday to Friday). Donations. For information call (408) 294-2787.

For fun, take the family to **Raging Waters**, 2333 White Road, Lake Cunningham Regional Park, ideal for restless youngsters, with more than 35 water attractions that include water slides.

An amazing true story is that of Sarah Winchester, heiress to the Winchester firearms fortune, who was so frightened of ghosts that she kept adding new rooms to her house to confuse the spirits. The bizarre mansion ended up with 160 rooms and 2,000 doors (many leading absolutely nowhere). There are daily guided tours through the mansion (the **Winchester Mystery House**) at 525 South Winchester Boulevard, and self-guided tours of the Victorian gardens and outbuildings. Also on the estate are the **Winchester Historic Firearms Museum** and **Antique Products Museum** featuring knives, tools and other artifacts. *Open*: 9:00A.M.–5:30P.M. (though times vary during the winter season). Admission charge (under-sixes free). For information call (408) 247-2101.

The **Technology Center of Silicon Valley**, at 145 West San Carlos opened in 1990 featuring hands-on exhibits of the past, present and future. *Open*: Tuesday to Sunday 10:00A.M.–5:00P.M.. Admission charge. For information call (408) 279-7150.

Children love the Great America theme park at Santa Clara

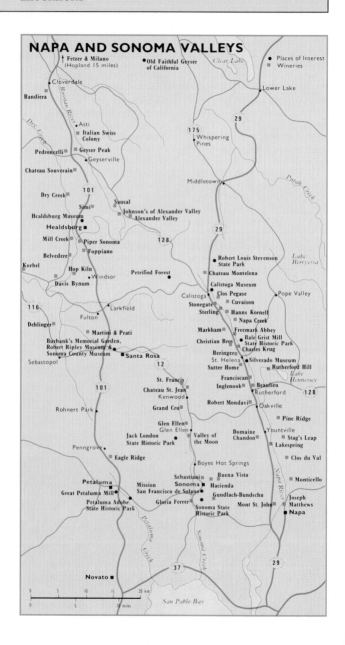

NAPA AND SONOMA VALLEYS

• Places of Interest
■ Wineries

Fetzer & Milano
(Hopland 15 miles)
Old Faithful Geyser
of California
Clear Lake

Cloverdale
Lower Lake

Bandiera

Russian River

Dry Creek

Asti
Italian Swiss
Colony

Pedroncelli
Geyser Peak
Geyserville

Chateau Souverain

Dry Creek
101

Middletown

175
Whispering
Pines

29

Putah Creek

Simi
Sausal
Johnson's of Alexander Valley
Alexander Valley

Healdsburg Museum

Healdsburg

Mill Creek
Piper Sonoma
128

29

Belvedere
Foppiano

Korbel
Hop Kiln

Davis Bynum
Windsor

Petrified Forest

Robert Louis Stevenson
State Park

Chateau Montelena

Calistoga Museum

Calistoga
Clos Pegase

Cuvaison

Lake
Berryessa

Pope Valley

116

Fulton
Larkfield

Stonegate
Sterling
Hanns Kornell
Napa Creek

Dehlinger

Markham
Freemark Abbey

Martini & Prati
Burbank's Memorial Garden,
Robert Ripley Museum &
Sonoma County Museum
Santa Rosa

Christian Bros
Bale Grist Mill
State Historic Park
Charles Krug

Beringers
St. Helena
Silverado Museum

Sebastopol

Sutter Home
Rutherford Hill

12

Franciscan

St. Francis

Inglenook
Beaulieu

Lake
Hennessey

Chateau St. Jean
Kenwood

Rutherford
128

101

Grand Cru

Robert Mondavi
Oakville

Rohnert Park

Pine Ridge

Glen Ellen
Glen Ellen

Domaine
Chandon
Yountville
Stag's Leap

Jack London
State Historic Park
Valley of
the Moon

Lakespring

Penngrove

Clos du Val

Eagle Ridge

Boyes Hot Springs

Petaluma

Sebastiani
Buena Vista

Monticello

Great Petaluma Mill

Mission
San Francisco de Solano
Sonoma
Hacienda

Petaluma Adobe
State Historic Park

Gloria Ferrer
Gundlach-Bundschu

Sonoma State
Historic Park

Joseph
Matthews
Napa

Mont St. John

Petaluma Creek

Sonoma Creek

Napa River

37

29

Novato

0   5   10   15   20 km
0   5   10 miles

San Pablo Bay

SANTA CRUZ

79 miles (127km) south of San Francisco

This is a lively youthful town with plenty to see and do. The beach here is safe and pleasant since Santa Cruz is more sheltered than other points along the coast and its **Beach Boardwalk** is a classic shoreside amusement park with an old wooden roller coaster, traditional merry-go-round, bumper cars and shooting galleries, an indoor minature golf course, cotton candy and all the rest of the fun.

Open: daily from 11:00A.M. in summer, weekends only in winter. Boardwalk entrance free, charges for amusement rides.

On the subject of fun, why not try the **Mystery Spot**, 2.5 miles (4km) north, on Market Street to Branciforte Drive. Here you will experience the phenomenon that makes it seem as if gravity is reversed.

Half-hour tours are available daily 9:30A.M.–5:00P.M..

For information call (408) 423-8897.

Six miles (9.5km) inland, **Roaring Camp and Big Trees Narrow-Gauge Railroad** reincarnates 1880s village life with an old-fashioned general store, depot and covered bridge and rides by steam train.

Open: daily throughout the year. The more serious-minded will head for the **Mission Santa Cruz**, Emmett Street and High Street, a scaled-down replica of the church and a portion of an old barracks that is a remnant of California's smallest mission, founded in 1791, as 12th in the chain. The chapel is open to visitors daily 9:00A.M.–5:00P.M..

For information call (408) 426-5686.

Or there is the **City Museum**, 1305 East Cliff Drive, showing regional history exhibits.

Open: Tuesday to Saturday 10:00A.M.-5:00P.M., Sunday noon–5:00P.M.. For information call (408) 429-3773.

The **Santa Cruz County Historical Trust Museum** is at 118 Cooper Street.

Open: Tuesday to Sunday noon–5:00P.M..

For information call (408) 429-3773.

The **Santa Cruz Lighthouse**, West Cliff Drive, contains a unique surfing museum,.

Open: Thursday to Monday noon–4:00P.M. (weather permitting).

The **Art Museum of Santa Cruz County** at 1543 Pacific Avenue displays contemporary art; re-opens summer 1992 (call (408) 429-1964).

Open: Tuesday to Sunday noon–5:00P.M.. Thursday 6:00–9:00P.M. Admission charge except Sunday.

There is no charge to visit the **Antonelli Begonia Gardens**, 2545 Capitola Road, blooming at their best in peak season August and September, though they remain open from June to November. Near **Natural Bridges State Park** (whose white sandy beach is popular for surfing, sun and fishing) the **Long Marine Laboratory**, 100 Shafer Road, is a facility of the University of California. The lab features tidepool animal touch tanks and aquarium and an 85-foot (26m) blue whale skeleton.

Open: Tuesday to Sunday

EXCURSIONS

1:00–4:00P.M. Donations welcome. For information call (408) 429-4308 or, on weekends, call (408) 429-4087.

◆◆◆
SONOMA VALLEY
48 miles (77km) north of San Francisco
This is a touring route (by itself or in conjunction with Napa) favored by wine-lovers. There are innumerable wineries in this region (see map page 58 and **Where to Drink**, page 81), which was given the name "Valley of the Moon" by writer Jack London. He used to live in the House of Happy Walls, now a commemorative museum in **Jack London State Historic Park** in Glen Ellen. The house itself contains many mementos and within the 803-acre (325-hectare) park are the charred ruins of Wolf House (the 26-room mansion built for the author but never lived in), his grave and the ranch where he lived, worked and died.
Open: daily 8:00A.M–sunset (museum, 10:00A.M–5:00P.M). Admission charge per car. For information call (707) 938-5216.
If you are touring this valley, you might well stop in **Healdsburg** where the **Healdsburg Museum**, 221 Matheson Street, shows outstanding historical displays relating to the town's heritage.
Open: Tuesday to Sunday noon–5:00P.M. Free. For information call (707) 431-3325.
You are almost bound to stop in **Petaluma** whose **Great Petaluma Mill** is a riverfront landmark containing an 1854

Mission San Francisco Solano at Sonoma, last of the Californian missions

warehouse, relics and antique machinery and a restored shop and restaurant complex. Petaluma is an offbeat but historic little town, noted for its iron-fronted buildings and Victorian homes which survived the 1906 earthquake. Take a self-guided walking tour of Petaluma Boulevard between East Washington and B Streets to see some of the best and also visit the **Historical Museum and Library**, 20 Fourth Street, where exhibits date from the 1850s and the 1906 library claims California's only freestanding stained-glass dome.
Open: Thursday to Monday 1:00–4:00P.M. Admission charge.
Petaluma Adobe State Historic Park on Adobe road is where General Vallejo's ranch has been restored to its 1840s appearance, with a number of displays including tanning, weaving and candle-making.
Open: 10:00A.M–5:00P.M. Admission charge but children under six free. Same-day tickets are good for visiting Sonoma Mission, Sonoma Barracks and the General M G Vallejo home. For information call (707) 762-4871).
Sonoma is the valley's main town, the site of the last of the Franciscan Missions, seat of the last Mexican government of upper California and locale for anti-Mexico rebels. Most of the buildings that recall that era are situated around Sonoma Plaza where **Sonoma State Historic Park** embraces the Mission San Francisco Solano, the barracks, the Mexican garrison and the scene of the 1846 Bear Flag Revolt, which was successful but

short lived. If you are hungry, stop on Spain Street at the Sonoma Cheese Factory – a country store where you can watch all types of Sonoma Jack cheese being made, and eat it, too.
Santa Rosa farther north could well be a chosen base for touring the valley the other way around. Botanist Luther Burbank certainly thought it was a perfect place to grow plants, and his **Home and Memorial Gardens**, on 415 Steele Lane, are well worth visiting. There are many personal memorabilia and original furnishings. Guided tours (every half hour) include a look at his greenhouse design and a description of his life and work.
House open: Wednesday to Sunday 10:00A.M.–4:00P.M., early-April to mid-October. Admission charge. *Gardens open*: daily during daylight hours. No charge.
In Juilliard Park at 492 Sonoma Avenue is the **Church of One Tree/Robert Ripley Memorial Museum** built from a single redwood and dedicated to the man who turned the words "Believe it or not" into a household phrase.
Open: Wednesday to Sunday, March to October 11:00A.M.–4:00P.M.. Admission charge (under-sixes free).
For information call (707) 576-5233.
The **Sonoma County Museum** housed in the restored 1909 Old Post Office Building, at 425 7th Street, displays a range of cultural and artistic exhibits.
Open: Wednesday to Sunday 11:00A.M.–4:00P.M.. Under-12s free.

PEACE AND QUIET

Wildlife and Countryside in and around San Francisco by Paul Sterry

Despite being a vast city, San Francisco has an excellent transportation network which allows easy exploration of central California. Within the boundaries of the city itself, and adjacent urban areas such as Berkeley and Oakland, there are still pockets of preserved, natural habitats. Further afield, a day trip could take you to some exciting coastline, such as Point Reyes to the north or Monterey to the south. Even the Yosemite National Park is less than a six-hour drive from the city. The Californian countryside around San Francisco holds plenty of interest for the visiting naturalist. Colorful spring flowers are a botanist's delight and birdwatching, especially around the marshes and shores, will yield thousands of birds, of many species, new even to birdwatchers from the eastern US. Sea otters and sea lions feed around the coast and, at certain times of the year, California gray whales and several other species of cetaceans can be seen on whale-watching tours, or even from coastal headlands. Whether you simply want to relax in beautiful surroundings or observe wildlife, a visit to San Francisco is rewarding.

Golden Gate Park

Golden Gate Park is a narrow, rectangular area of land which lies just to the south of the bridge from which it gains its name. The park's lakes are the haunt of numerous ducks, while the flower borders and well-managed woodlands harbor butterflies, moths and an interesting range of birds. Although the lakes are mainly the haunt of wildfowl such as mallard, wood duck, ring-necked duck, American wigeon, canvasback and ruddy duck, several species of gulls can also be found. Migrant landbirds can be seen in spring and autumn and resident species include pygmy nuthatch, scrub jay and bushtit. The western boundary of the park is marked by the Pacific Ocean, which offers a rewarding alternative to the park's wildlife. Along the shoreline and on the offshore Sea Rocks, wading birds such as surfbird, black oystercatcher, willet and black turnstone may be seen in autumn and winter, together with brown pelicans and Heerman's gulls. Sooty shearwaters sometimes feed out at sea, and between December and April there is a chance of seeing migrating California gray whales.

Lake Merritt

Lake Merritt lies in Oakland on the east side of San Francisco Bay and is the haunt of thousands of water birds. Winter is the best season, but there is plenty to see throughout the year. Ducks are the most numerous birds, and flocks may comprise ruddy duck, mallard, pintail, goldeneye, Barrow's goldeneye, canvasback and red-breasted merganser. Occasionally, herons and egrets are seen on the shores while

Grey phalaropes feed on the saltwater Lake Merritt at Oakland

Thayer's gulls, western gulls,
California gulls and glaucous-
winged gulls remain alert for
morsels of food. Wilson's and
grey phalaropes also swim
buoyantly across the water,
looking more like miniature
gulls than the waders they
really are.

Lake Merced
Lake Merced can be found near
San Francisco State University –
which is near the Pacific Ocean.
Grebes, divers, cormorants,
gulls, terns and ducks such as
pintail, shoveler, American
wigeon and ring-necked duck
can be seen in large numbers.
Migrating phalaropes
sometimes stop off to feed on
the lake.

The Coast and Sea
The San Francisco area is richly
endowed with beautiful
coastline. Sandy beaches, rocky
shores and dramatic cliffs run
from Point Reyes south to
Monterey, and San Francisco
Bay and San Pablo Bay still hold
saltmarshes and mudflats. The
birdlife is abundant and varied
both around the coast and out to
sea, and California's remarkable
variety of marine mammals is
one of the wildlife highlights of
an enjoyable trip to San
Francisco.
Shorebirds are an outstanding
feature of the coast and are
especially fun to watch during
spring and autumn migration.
Regular species include willet,
ruddy turnstone, black

PEACE AND QUIET

oystercatcher, surfbird and marbled godwit and these may be joined by spotted sandpipers, dunlin, least sandpipers, western sandpipers and many others. Saltmarshes, comprising glasswort (pickleweed), may harbor the elusive black rail, while freshwater marshes, comprising reed-mace (cattail) and reeds, are the haunt of herons and egrets.

Offshore, brown pelicans, double-crested cormorants and several species of gulls and terns can be seen; while truly pelagic birds (birds of the open ocean) sometimes come close during periods of onshore winds. The best way to see these birds, however, is to go on one of the special pelagic trips that operate out of harbors from Bodega Bay to Monterey Bay. The latter is a particularly rewarding marine area, because the edge of the continental shelf, a rich feeding ground for birds and mammals, lies comparatively close to shore.

Biological Journeys and **Dolphin Charters** operate a wide range of trips around the San Francisco Bay wilderness area and offshore from November until May. Trips offer the guidance of professional naturalists, which is extremely helpful. Call (800) 548-7555 (toll free), (707) 839-0178 or 527-9622 for details.

As you move away from the shore, sea otters float in the kelp

Female Californian sea lion: these intelligent mammals haunt the Bay

beds, seals and Californian sea lions will be seen and Dall's porpoises sometimes ride the bow-wave of the boats. In general, more sea birds are seen as you travel away from land. There are thousands of sooty shearwaters, together with smaller numbers of pink-footed shearwaters, pomarine and Arctic skuas and the occasional black-footed albatross and red-billed tropicbird.

The highlight of these pelagic trips is undoubtedly the whales. Blue whales, the largest animals ever to have lived, are regularly seen, and humpback whales feed on the abundant marine life. Beside the blue whale, the humpback is comparatively small and buoyant and often raises its flipper or tail well out of the water. Best known, however, are the California gray whales which migrate south past San Francisco in December and January and north again in March and April. Each year, these amazingly fearless animals swim from their feeding grounds in the Arctic to their calving grounds in the coastal lagoons of Baja California in Mexico, and lines of spouting whales can sometimes even be seen from the shore.

Muir Woods National Monument
This area comprises over 500 acres (200 hectares) of forests of coastal redwoods, which lie north of the Golden Gate Bridge on State 1. The immense trees are among the most impressive to be seen anywhere in the world. Brown creepers and

Steller's jays inhabit these woods, but because of the height of the trees, birdwatching soon leads to neck strain. At ground level, California quails provide more relaxed viewing as they forage among the ground vegetation.

Golden Gate National Recreation Area
Lying on the north side of the Golden Gate, the recreation area comprises coastal woodland, sandy beaches and dramatic headlands, all set against a backdrop of the Golden Gate Bridge and the city of San Francisco. Resident birds, mammals and insects are numerous, and this is also a good area to watch the bird migration, in particular of birds of prey, with autumn being the best season. Fog often defeats the observer, but when it clears, hawks, band-tailed pigeons and swifts will soon appear in considerable numbers.

Redwood Regional Park
Not to be confused with the magnificent Redwood National Park in the north of California (see page 46), Redwood Regional Park lies to the east of Oakland, a short distance from San Francisco. It comprises a mixture of habitats, including woodland with magnificent redwood trees, meadows and scrub. Birdlife is typical of lowland woodland in California and the mammals, insects and plants are varied.

Sharp-eyed observers may see a saw-whet owl perched among the branches of the redwoods, while brown creepers, hairy woodpeckers and red-breasted

PEACE AND QUIET

Trillium ovatum: *this lily-like flower is native to the western US*

nuthatches investigate the bark in search of insects and spiders. Breeding songbirds include Hutton's vireo and Swainson's thrush, which are much less conspicuous than the park's brightly colored Steller's jays. Bright swallowtail butterflies fly gracefully along paths and roads and often look more impressive, in terms of size, than the Allen's hummingbirds, which also visit the woods.

Point Reyes National Seashore
Point Reyes and adjacent Tomales Bay State Park lie less than 40 miles (65km) to the north of San Francisco and provide a wonderful setting for a relaxing day's escape from the city. Sandy beaches pounded by Pacific breakers contrast with dramatic cliffs, which offer spectacular views along the coast. Inland, flower-rich meadows and wooded valleys are kept lush and moist by the dense fogs which frequently shroud the peninsula. Both the seashore and woodland wildlife of the area are fascinating, and if a single day's visit does not seem long enough, campsites allow you to extend your stay. The rocky headland of Point Reyes is home to guillemots, pigeon guillemots and Brandt's cormorants, which nest here in late spring. Gulls such as

California, western, Thayer's and Bonaparte's gulls scavenge along the beaches, while offshore, great northern divers, red-throated divers, red-necked grebes, surf scoters, red-breasted mergansers and many others can be seen riding the waves. California sea lions and elephant seals roll in the water and sometimes haul out onto rocks to bask, while, out to sea, the spouts of California gray whales are occasionally seen during the migration between December and April. If you follow the "Earthquake Trail," along part of the San Andreas Fault, to the Point Reyes lighthouse, you will find the ideal perch for whale-watching in season.

During spring and summer, grassy meadows are full of butterflies and colorful flowers such as milkweeds, paintbrush and blennosperma, the latter sometimes forming rich, yellow carpets. Fields are the haunt of birds such as western kingbird, Say's phoebe, western meadowlark and mourning dove, while loggerhead shrikes and crows eagerly watch for food from vantage points such as branches or posts. During migration time in spring and autumn a wide variety of birds may be seen, but the exact species vary from day to day. The moist air encourages an interesting ground flora in the coastal woodlands. Several species of orchids grow alongside a profusion of flowers of western trillium, snow queen and penstemon. Squirrels, California ground squirrels, Swainson's thrushes and

California quails often feed on the ground while, in the branches above, western flycatchers, northern pygmy owls, chestnut-backed chickadees and western bluebirds can be seen. Vaux's swifts hunt for insects over the treetops, while the tiny Allen's hummingbird visits woodland glades to feed on nectar.
For further information about the park call park headquarters at 663-1092.

Gulf of the Farallones National Marine Sanctuary

This protected marine environment extends from the coastline just north of the city to encircle the Farallon Islands 27 miles (43km) offshore and is a nationally recognized marine habitat. The island chain itself is the largest seabird breeding rookery between British Columbia and Mexico – more than 300,000 birds representing 12 species live and breed here. For information call 556-3509.

Yosemite National Park

Yosemite is undoubtedly California's most famous national park and is one of the best known wilderness areas in North America. This reputation is justly deserved. The scenery is stunning, the wildlife of the Sierra Nevada is rich and varied and the park has an excellent network of paths and trails which will suit the needs of both the casual visitor and the more serious outdoor enthusiast and naturalist. A free shuttle bus service operates in Yosemite Valley, passing most valley trail heads.
The focal point of the national

park is the Yosemite Valley, flanked by amazing water cascades and rock formations such as Bridalveil Falls, El Capitan and Half Dome. During the summer, this valley is generally thronged with day-trippers and many of the shorter trails are popular. However, venture a little way from any parking lot and you are more likely to find comparative peace and quiet, with only the trees, birds and mammals of Yosemite and the occasional like-minded person to keep you company. After Labor Day, the overwhelming numbers of visitors to Yosemite drop off, and autumn is a great time to go there.

One result of the enormous crowds of visitors to park is that many of the mammals and birds have become quite accustomed to human presence. Ground squirrels and mule deer are tame, and black bears sometimes show an alarming interest in campers' provisions. Robins, Steller's jays and juncos visit campsites and picnic areas and are almost indifferent to people, except, of course, when those people offer scraps of food.

Fast flowing rivers throughout Yosemite are the haunt of dippers, belted kingfishers and spotted sandpipers, while shrubs and bushes may harbor warbling vireos, Wilson's warblers, Nashville warblers and a variety of sparrows and flycatchers. Pileated woodpeckers, Williamson's sapsuckers and acorn woodpeckers investigate the trunks and branches of the trees, and the lucky observer may even see a saw-whet owl or great horned owl sitting immobile overhead. Meadows and clearings such as Tuolumne Meadows are full of colorful flowers such as paintbrush and penstemon and are sometimes visited by Calliope hummingbirds.

Call (209) 372-4845 for recorded information on roads, weather conditions, camping and recreation. Information is also posted at park entrances.

Kings Canyon and Sequoia National Parks

These two national parks lie adjacent to one another and stretch for over 60 miles (96km) along the western slopes of the Sierra Nevada. They are reached via State 198, which takes you up from the low-lying San Joaquin Valley into the hills and mountains. As you climb through the parks, the scenery becomes more impressive, the beauty due in no small part to the stately trees that grow here. At around 6,000 ft (1,800m) you begin to see giant sequoias, which are among the most stunning trees to be seen anywhere in the world. Groves of these giants will take your breath away and invariably lead to an aching neck, especially if you are a birdwatcher. Fortunately, there are many smaller species such as dogwood, willow, oak, fir and cottonwood which harbor interesting species such as warbling vireo, golden-crowned kinglet and orange-crowned warbler.

Squirrels, chipmunks, black

The glacier-carved canyon of the Yosemite Valley with Bridalveil Falls and El Capitan rock formations

bears and mountain quail forage on the forest floor searching for fruits, berries and nuts. The forest glades ring to the sounds of pileated woodpeckers and yellow-bellied sapsuckers, and Cassin's finches and, in the evening, grosbeaks feed among the higher branches.

To the east of Kings Canyon lie the White Mountains, home to bristlecone pines, many of which are thousands of years old and among the oldest living things. The Shulman Grove at Westguard Pass is perhaps the best place to see these gnarled and ancient trees.

The parks are open all year, but the more remote areas become inaccessible in winter. The admission charge is per vehicle or per person entering by other means. Bus tours operate daily during summer. Mules and horses may be rented.

Call (209) 561-3314 for park information.

Mono Lake

Mono Lake lies about seven hours southeast of San Francisco, close to the Nevada border. It is an area of extraordinary beauty: the formations of tufa give it the appearance of a moonscape, which is most stunning at dawn and dusk. Large numbers of birds nest here, and the aquatic life in the saline waters attracts thousands of migrant waders each spring and autumn.

Mono Lake is at the center of considerable environmental controversy. The tufa formations, for which it is famous, are more and more at risk from a drop in water level. This is due to the diversion of the Leevining River, which once fed the lake, to supply part of the water requirements of Los Angeles. The formations are being eroded by wind and rain, but also at risk is the large colony of California gulls and black-necked grebes.

The sagebrush which surrounds the lake is full of wildlife. Rattlesnakes and small mammals scurry through the vegetation and birds such as sage thrasher, pinyon jay, sage sparrow and bushtit can be found. In spring, sage grouse perform their elaborate courtship displays, watched over by kestrels and loggerhead shrikes.

Western diamond-backed rattlesnake, not dangerous unless provoked

FOOD AND DRINK

Eating Out

Eating out in San Francisco is a true pleasure and a gourmet one at that (ever since "Diamond" Jim Brady downed six dozen oysters at The Palace Hotel). There are countless restaurants to choose from, whether they be cheap take-out or fast food outlets or world-class silver service fine dining. Thanks to favorable weather, many are al fresco, by the waterfront or overlooking the Bay.

There are coffee shops and chic continental-style cafés; brasseries and bistros; tavernas and trattorias. You name it and you will find it, for the city has never been short of an eclectic ethnic mix. So many immigrants from other parts of the world settled in San Francisco that all types of cuisine are available. The Italians were particularly intent on opening restaurants so pasta and pizza parlors are plentiful. They even call the North Beach area Little Italy. If *sushi* and *sake* are your cup of green tea, Japantown is the place with its focal point, the Japanese Cultural and Trade Center.

Of all the ethnic groups whose food has become popular here, most outstanding is the Chinese. Chinatown is not just a tourist attraction, but a vibrant community filled with Chinese grocery shops, tiny hole-in-the-wall cheap eateries selling *dim sum* and some of the city's best restaurants where a spread is a banquet.

Vegetarians should be pleased since fresh fruit, vegetables and nuts have made California famous, and for fish-lovers San Francisco is notable for the freshest of seafood. You can buy plump pink shrimps along with Dungeness crabs and clams by the carton from kiosks down at Fisherman's Wharf or eat them elsewhere in style. Try abalone, which, though it is a shellfish, is nothing like any other shellfish you may have sampled. If you order tuna, don't automatically expect it to come straight from a can – in San Francisco it is quite often fresh. Several kinds of seafood go into the speciality dish known as *cioppino*, San Francisco's

Seafood fanatics are well cared for

FOOD AND DRINK

answer to a bouillabaisse. And the accompaniment *must* be sourdough bread.

Meat-eaters will be just as delighted, for steak is as prized as fish. The "San Francisco Steak House" has become a term used for a style of décor around the globe, authentically simulating the old-style saloon with lots of red plush. Cattle used to be the mainstay of California and, before there were towns and rail tracks, there were great ranches whose owners were known as Silver Dons for their silver adornments.

In keeping with the fanciful décor, San Francisco chefs are innovative enough to have created concoctions like Green Goddess salad dressing, to mix fruit with greens as a tasty salad and, while not being inventors of Polynesian fare, at least to give it an American stamp of approval – the very first Trader Vic's opened here. Frankly there are no set hours for eating other than a restaurant's own opening and closing ones. And there are plenty of tempting spots at which to enjoy weekend brunch, usually from 11:00A.M. to 3:00P.M., often offered for a fixed price, and including a Bloody Mary or mimosa (champagne and orange juice) and presented with a flourish. Saturday or Sunday brunch can be a way of cutting out one meal of the day, especially in the hotels where the spread is lavish. Many restaurants also offer special price early bird dinners before 7:00P.M. – a good idea if you're hungry, want to save a little money and plan to spend the later hours walking along the moonlit pier.

What follows is a selection of restaurants from the 4,300-odd which the city has to offer – from elegant to family style, and with service perhaps at cloud level, below ground, al fresco or afloat.

Restaurants with a View

A skyscraper setting where dinner and cocktails come with the view is not so hard to find in San Francisco. Here are a few.

Carnelian Room (52nd floor), Bank of America Building, 555 California Street (tel: 433-7500). The cuisine and prestige are considered by many to be worth the expense, and if the full spread is too much for the wallet, try Sunday brunch or cocktails in the Pacific Room. Expensive.

Crown Room of the Fairmont Hotel (24th floor), 950 Mason Street, Nob Hill (tel: 772-5131). Offers a buffet lunch, dinners in style and Sunday brunch. Moderate prices.

Equinox, Hyatt Regency Hotel (18th floor), 5 Embarcadero Center (tel: 778-1234). The city's only revolving rooftop restaurant for an everchanging view from your table. Moderate prices.

Henri's, San Francisco Hilton and Tower (46th floor), 333 O'Farrell Street (tel: 771-1400). Offers nightly entertainment and is also open for lunch.

Hugo's One Up, Hyatt Hotel (36th floor), Union Square (tel: 398-1234). Serves lunch, dinner and Sunday brunch with background piano music.

Starlite Roof, Sir Francis Drake

Hotel (21st floor), 450 Powell Street (tel: 392-7755). An elegant "must" with cocktails and dancing.

Top of the Mark at the Mark Hopkins Inter-Continental Hotel, 1 Nob Hill (tel: 392-3434). Traditional Sunday buffet brunch. Cocktails daily. Moderate prices.

Victor's, Westin St Francis Hotel (32nd floor), 335 Powell Street, Union Square (tel: 956-7777). Champagne adds sparkle to Sunday brunch. Dinners also served. Expensive. **Oz** on the same floor keeps the drinks coming from as early as 4:30P.M. and the dance music going until 3:00A.M. on weekends.

Waterfront Establishments

San Francisco's colorful waterfront is immediately atmospheric and in this city you can dine alongside or overlooking it. Fisherman's Wharf is an ideal location to start and not surprisingly many eating places here specialize in seafood.

Alioto's No 8, 8 Fisherman's Wharf (tel: 673-0183). The oldest restaurant on the Wharf with spectacular views and continental/seafood cuisine. Moderate prices.

Dante's Sea Catch, Pier 39 (tel: 421-5778). Fantastic view, a cozy atmosphere and fresh seafood and Italian dishes on the menu. Moderate prices.

Eagle Café, Pier 39 (tel: 433-3689). American fare – a favorite since 1928. Breakfast and lunch only. Inexpensive.

Franciscan, Pier 43½,

Fisherman's Wharf is a favorite area for enjoying a relaxed meal while watching the world go by

FOOD AND DRINK

Embarcadero (tel: 362-7733). Offers lunch and dinner while you view the Bay and its islands and eat seafood. Moderate prices.

Neptune's Palace, Pier 39 (tel: 434-2260). Features superb fresh seafood for lunch, dinner and weekend brunches with unsurpassable Bay views. Moderate prices.

Old Swiss House, Pier 39 (tel: 434-0432). Adds a Swiss French touch, with French cooking and chalet décor, to a fabulous view overlooking the fishing boats. Moderate prices.

Paprikas Fono, Ghirardelli Square, 900 North Point (tel: 441-1223). On an upper-level you can enjoy a dash of paprika and a plate of goulash – an authentic Hungarian experience with a view. Moderate prices.

Vanelli's, Pier 39 (tel: 421-7261). Prepares fresh seafood the continental way for lunch, dinner and weekend brunches, and again the Bay view is superb. Moderate prices.

Seafood

Even without a spectacular view, San Francisco's seafood restaurant are very fine. Some recommendations follow.

Chic's Place, Pier 39, Fisherman's Wharf (tel: 421-2442). A seafood grill and bar (even serves breakfast Monday to Saturday and Sunday brunch) in a bistro-type setting. Moderate prices.

Nautilus, Pier 39, Fisherman's Wharf (tel: 433-3721) serves good fish at the best price. Inexpensive.

Pompei's Grotto, 340 Jefferson Street (tel: 776-9265). Established

over 40 years ago and favored by locals. Moderate prices.

Rusty Scupper, 1800 Montgomery Street (tel: 986-1180). A waterfront restaurant with an oyster bar. Moderate prices.

Scott's Seafood Grill and Bar, 3 Embarcadero Center and also at 2400 Lombard Street. No reservations at this popular restaurant. Moderate prices.

Classy Continental

Amelio's, 1630 Powell Street (tel: 397-4339). It has won enough awards for excellent food to warrant its high prices. The location is North Beach which probably accounts for the Italian flavor in this intimate and romantic restaurant. Expensive.

Blue Fox, 659 Merchant Street (tel: 981-1177). A restaurant name that has been respected for many years and one of San Francisco's most elegant dining venues. Northern Italian cuisine. Expensive.

Ernie's, 847 Montgomery Street (tel: 397-5969). Plush Victorian elegance and serving food French-style with exquisite wines. Expensive.

Several of the top hotels have highly rated dining rooms that offer silver service and sophisticated continental dishes, most notably the Fairmont's **Venetian Room** and the Hyatt on Union Square's **Hugo's One Up** (see page 72).

American Fare

Houlihan's Old Place, The Anchorage, Fisherman's Wharf (tel: 775-7523). The name may sound Irish but Houlihan's serves more eclectic fare, from

FOOD AND DRINK

Elegant luxury is the hallmark of the Empress of China restaurant which sets it apart from many other restaurants

salads to burgers to Sunday brunch, plus nightly dancing. As they say, a place for everyone, offering a limitless variety. Inexpensive.

Maye's Original Oyster House, 1233 Polk Street (tel: 474-7674). You know just what to expect in San Francisco's second oldest restaurant. Moderate prices.

Perry's, 1944 Union Street (tel: 922-9022). A New York-style saloon serving breakfast, lunch and dinner until midnight. It also serves weekend brunch. No reservations necessary. Inexpensive.

Phil Lehr's Steakery, San Francisco Hilton, 330 Taylor Street (tel: 673-6800). Your steaks are cut to order and you pay by the ounce.

Chinese

Cathay House, 718 California Street (tel: 982-3388). One of Chinatown's best known restaurants, it has been a landmark since 1938, overlooking Grant Avenue. Moderate prices.

Celadon, 881 Clay Street (tel: 982-1168). Serves award-winning Chinese food right from a wheeled cart. Moderate prices.

Empress of China, China Trade Center Building (6th floor), 838 Grant Avenue (tel: 434-1345). The luxurious décor sets it apart from other places, and flaming young quail is one of the specialties. Moderate prices.

Far East, 631 Grant Avenue (tel: 982-3245). Has private booths for more intimate dining. Moderate prices.

Golden Dragon, 816 Washington Street (tel: 398-3920). *Dim sum* lunches; dinners daily. Inexpensive.

Golden Phoenix, 728 Washington Street (tel: 989-4400). Order Peking duck in

FOOD AND DRINK

advance (it is superb). Moderate prices.

Grand Palace, 950 Grant Avenue (tel: 982-3705). Good value *dim sum* and traditional Chinese food. Moderate prices.

Imperial Palace, 919 Grant Avenue (tel: 982-4440). Chinatown's most exclusive restaurant. Expensive.

Kan's, 708 Grant Avenue (tel: 982-2388). Delicious Cantonese fare. Moderate prices.

Mandarin, Ghirardelli Square, 900 North Point (tel: 673-8812). Highly rated for Szechwan and Shanghai cuisine. Moderate prices.

Yank Sing, 427 Battery Street (tel: 362-1640) and 49 Stevenson Street (tel: 495-4510). Noted for its *dim sum*. Inexpensive.

Yet Wah, Pier 39, Fisherman's Wharf (tel: 434-4430). Serves fine dishes from every part of China. Moderate prices.

Italian
Albona Ristorante Istriano, 545 Francisco Street, North Beach (tel: 441-1040). Offers a mixture of northern Italian and central European dishes – rich and spicy. Moderate prices.

Circolo Restaurant and Champagneria, 161 Sutter Street (tel: 362-0404). Features a range of Italian specialties. Moderate prices.

Enoteca Lanzone's, Civic Center, 601 Van Ness Avenue (tel: 928-0400). Art gallery-like restaurant serving excellent pasta. Moderate prices.

Fior d'Italia, 601 Union Street, North Beach (tel: 986-1886). Northern Italian dishes. Moderate prices.

Il Padrino, 622 Green Street, North Beach (tel: 778-1299).

Fior d'Italia. San Francisco has a good choice of Italian restaurants

Sicilian and Italian specialties. Moderate prices.

Iron Horse, 19 Maiden Lane (tel: 362-8133). A quiet retreat offering northern Italian specialties. Moderate prices.

Magic Flute, 3673 Sacramento Street, Presidio Heights (tel: 922-1225). Changes its menu of home-cooked pasta, seafood, veal dishes and desserts daily. Moderate prices.

Marina Café, 2417 Lombard Street (tel: 929-7241). Often recommended by residents as the best in town. Moderate prices.

Martinelli's, 532 Columbus Avenue, North Beach (tel: 391-3800). A lively setting in which to enjoy Italian favorites. Moderate prices.

New San Remo, 2237 Mason Street, North Beach (tel: 673-9090). Northern Italian cuisine in a Victorian décor. Moderate prices.

North Beach Restaurant, 1512 Stockton Street, North Beach (tel: 392-1700). Home-style northern Italian cooking. Moderate prices.

Prego, 2000 Union Street (tel: 563-3305). A sophisticated trattoria serving spit-roasted meats and pizzas from an oak-burning oven. Moderate prices.

Trattoria Contadina, 1800 Mason Street, North Beach (tel: 982-5728). Authentic regional specialties. Inexpensive.

Umberto Ristorante, 141 Steuart Street, Embarcadero (tel: 543-8021). Florentine cuisine excels here. Moderate prices.

French

Brasserie Chambord, 150 Kearny Street (tel: 434-3688). Popular lunch spot in the financial district. Moderate prices.

Lafayette on Pacific, 290 Pacific Avenue (tel: 986-3366). Vaguely *nouvelle*-ish food. Has a piano bar. Moderate prices.

La Mère Duquesne, 101 Shannon Alley, Union Square (tel: 776-7600). Simple elegance as the setting for French country cooking. Moderate prices.

La Quiche, 550 Taylor Street, Union Square (tel: 441-2711). Just a friendly little bistro. Inexpensive to moderate.

Lascaux, 250 Sutter Street, Union Square (tel: 391-1555). Rustic French fare and sometimes live jazz make this cellar restaurant interesting. Moderate prices.

L'Etoile, 1075 California Street, Nob Hill (tel: 771-1529). Preferred by the socially élite. Has a piano bar too. Expensive.

L'Olivier, 465 Davis Court, Embarcadero (tel: 981-7824). Fresh flowers and antique sideboards complement the fine cuisine in this quiet retreat. Moderate prices.

Rotunda Restaurant, 150 Stockton Street (tel: 362-4777). Serves up true *nouvelle cuisine* under its glass dome. Moderate prices.

European Mix

Whatever you fancy you will find.

Beethoven Restaurant (German), 1701 Powell Street, North Beach (tel: 391-4488). The roast goose and Wienerschnitzel are classically prepared. Moderate prices.

Little Spain Restaurant and Bar (Spanish), 1333 Columbus Avenue, Fisherman's Wharf (tel: 673-3273). Paella and tapas with

FOOD AND DRINK

a Californian tinge. Moderate
prices.
Square One Restaurant
(Mediterranean), 190 Pacific
Avenue, Embarcadero (tel: 788-
1110). Brings together the tastes
of several Mediterranean
countries – European and
Middle Eastern. Moderate
prices.

Eastern Mix
Fujiya (Japanese), 1
Embarcadero Center, lobby
level (tel: 398-1151). A *teppan*
steak and seafood house with
sushi and *shabu-shabu* bars.
Moderate prices.
Ichirin (Japanese), 330 Mason
Street, Union Square (tel: 956-
6085). Not only tempts with *sushi*
but also boasts a *tempura* bar

Japanese Tea Gardens

and *tatami* room where music is
played nightly. Moderate prices.
Padang (Indonesian), 700 Post
Street, Union Square (tel: 775-
6708). Recommended for true
Indonesian spreads. Moderate
prices.
Raffles (Polynesian), 1390
Market Street, Civic Center (tel:
621-8601). Offerings include
exotic rum drinks and curries.
Thai Inspiration (Thai), 1217
Sutter Street (tel: 441-5003). One
of the city's better Thai
restaurants. Moderate prices.
Yamato Restaurant (Japanese),
717 California Street, Chinatown
(tel: 397-3456). Fine food served
by a kimono-clad waitress.
Moderate prices.

Spicy Food
Mexican rates strongly in this
bracket. Among the better
restaurants are the following.
Cadillac Bar, One Holland Court
(tel: 543-8226). Dinner may be
ordered until midnight and
mariachis play under ceiling
fans. Moderate prices.
La Posada, 2298 Fillmore Street,
Pacific Heights (tel: 922-1722).
One of the best Mexican places.
Offers lunch, dinner and Sunday
brunch. Inexpensive.
Gaylord India, Ghirardelli
Square (tel: 771-8822) and at
One Embarcadero Center (tel:
397-7775). Of the Indian eating
places, no one can fault this
restaurant. It features mouth-
watering curries and tandoori
dishes from the clay oven.

Californian
California Café Bar and Grill,
50 Broadway, Embarcadero (tel:
433-4400). Outdoor dining and
piano music are featured.

Moderate prices.

Ivy's Restaurant and Bar, 398 Hayes Street (tel: 626-3930). A favorite Civic Center hangout, featuring a daily changing menu. Moderate prices.

Tuba Garden, 3634 Sacramento Street (tel: 921-TUBA). Lunch and brunch only can be enjoyed in a garden setting adorned by local artist's work. Inexpensive.

Inexpensive

There is plenty to choose from in this category. The cheapest establishments are often Far Eastern in cuisine (Chinese, Japanese or Thai). In the Chinatown area you can find the following restaurants.

Canton Tea House, 1108 Stockton Street (tel: 982-1032). A prime example of a family-style restaurant that features *dim sum* and dishes in clay pots at easy-on-the-budget prices.

Golden Dragon, 816 Washington Street (tel: 398-3920).

Gum Tong, 675 Jackson Street (tel: 788-5393).

Hang Ah Tea Room, 1 Hang Ah Street (tel: 982-5686). A small café near the Chinese playground, serving authentic *dim sum* in a cheap and cheerful way.

Ocean City, 640 Broadway (tel: 982-2328). There is an extensive menu and a nightclub here.

Some Japanese restaurants feature *karioke* bars, where anyone can get up and sing.

Hime, 336 O'Farrell Street (tel: 441-4756). Boasts a *karioke* bar and plenty of *sushi* as well.

Sushi Boat, 389 Geary Street (tel: 781-5111). *Sushi* and other Japanese specialties reach diners via miniature boats. Inexpensive Thai food suggestions follow.

Bangkok Palace, 760 Broadway (tel: 421-0875).

Franthai, 939 Kearny Street (tel: 397-3543).

Cheap Mexican food is available at the following places.

Compadres Mexican Bar and Grill, Ghirardelli Square, Fisherman's Wharf (tel: 885-2266). Sautées, stews and grills are part of the full range of Mexican specialties on the menu here.

Don Ramon's, 225 11th Street, Civic Center (tel: 864-2700). Tacos, tortillas and enchiladas galore are on the menu.

La Barca, 2036 Lombard Street (tel: 921-2221). Traditional Mexican food has been served here for years.

Margaritaville, 1787 Union Street (tel: 441-1183). Rock music and magnificent margaritas made with tequila are the plus factors here, and colorful murals and videos add to the festive atmosphere.

Pepe's, Pier 39, Fishermen's Wharf (tel: 434-1818). Open daily from 11:00A.M.. Mexican specialties with a view.

For pizzas and other Italian-style snacks try the following.

Caffe Quadro, 180 Pacific Avenue (tel: 398-1777). Good for homemade sandwiches and pizzas.

Columbus, 611 Broadway (tel: 781-2939). An Italian family business that cooks to order and produces what many locals say is the city's best calamari.

Pizzeria Uno, 2323 Powell Street, North Point (tel: 788-

FOOD AND DRINK

Eat 1950s-style, with fast food and counter service at Lori's Diner

4055) and at 2200 Lombard Street (tel: 563-3144).

Spuntino, 524 Van Ness Avenue, Civic Center (tel: 861-7772). Quick bites that include oven-baked pizza, panini and pastries, and espresso coffee, are available to consume there or take out.

Vicolo Pizzeria, Ghirardelli Square (tel: 776-1331) and at 201 Ivy Street, Civic Center (tel: 863-2382).

Good value for money on, burgers and other diner fare is found at the following.

Hard Rock Café, 1699 Van Ness Avenue (tel: 885-1699).

Lori's Diner, 336 Mason Street (tel: 392-8646). Thick burgers and shakes are first rate in a 1950s-style atmosphere.

Max's Diner, 311 Third Street, Moscone Center (tel: 546-

MAXS). 1950s style with a soda fountain.

Zim's, 1498 Market Street (tel: 431-0600) and at Sutter and Powell Streets, Union Square (tel: 982-0900). Open 24 hours but does not serve alcohol.

Here are more cheap eateries.

The Crêpe Escape, 150 Kearny Street (tel: 434-3688). If you love French crêpes, they prepare them well here.

David's Delicatessen, 474 Geary Street (tel: 431-7337). A theater district deli that serves all day.

Magic Pan, 341 Sutter Street (tel: 788-7397) and at Ghirardelli Square, 900 North Point (tel: 474-6733). Crêpes and more at reasonable prices.

Salmagundi, 1236 Market Street (tel: 431-7337), with branches at 442 Geary Street (tel: 441-0894) and 2 Embarcadero Center (tel: 982-5603). An inexpensive souperie.

Where to Drink

San Francisco is full of bars, pubs and cocktail lounges, but in most cases they are attached to restaurants or hotels, or certainly all the famous ones are. Favorite watering holes invariably have a view (skyrooms or waterfront, see restaurant listings). Remember that some establishments only have a wine and beer license and some serve no alcohol. Two are worth mentioning. **Buena Vista**, 2765 Hyde Street (tel: 474-5044). A Wharf eating spot, but famous for its Irish coffee. **Trader Vic's**, 20 Cosmo Place (tel: 776-2232). Famous for its exotic cocktails.

On the Wine Trail

Wine drinking is a serious business out West and nearly all the coastal vineyard valleys lie within a day's drive of San Francisco. Practically all the wineries offer tours and tastings, either for free of for a nominal charge without need of an appointment. The most popular wine tour areas are the Napa and Sonoma Valleys. The following Napa wineries are particularly recommended. **Beringer Vineyards**, 2000 Main Street, St Helena (tel: 707) 963-4812). Produces many excellent wines. Its Rhenish house and tunnel network makes tours interesting. Open 9:30A.M.– 5:00P.M.. Tours daily. **Christian Brothers**, 2555 Main Street, St Helena (tel: 707) 963-0763). Famous and reliable wine name

with interesting Greystone cellars. Open daily 10:00A.M.–4:30P.M. (4:00P.M. in winter). **Domaine Chandon**, West California Drive, Yountville (tel: (707) 944-2280). Produces some of California's most stylish sparkling wines as an offshoot of Moët et Chandon should. Fabulous restaurant on the grounds. Winery open daily 11:00A.M.–6:00P.M. but closed Monday and Tuesday November–April. **Ingelnook**, 1991 St Helena Highway, Rutherford (tel: (707) 967-3359). Well-known name producing broad range of wines at all prices. Open daily for tastings and tours 10:00A.M.–5:00P.M.. **Robert Mondavi**, 7801 St Helena Highway, Oakville (tel: (707) 963-9611). Notable for its Cabernet Sauvignon. Excellent tours and very modern winery behind Spanish colonial façade. Open daily 9:00A.M.–5:00P.M. (10:00A.M.–4:40P.M. November– April). **Sterling**, 1111 Dunaweal Lane, Calistoga (tel: (707) 942-5151). Self-guided tours once you take the trolley to the top of a hill where the winery perches. Open daily 10:30A.M.–4:30P.M.. The following Sonoma wineries are excellent. **Buena Vista**, 18000 Old Winery Road, Sonoma (tel: (707) 938-1266). Famous as the oldest winery north of the city. Open daily 10:00A.M.–5:00P.M. with tastings and self-guided tour of wine caves. **Chateau St Jean**, 8555 Sonoma Highway, Kenwood (tel: (707) 833-4134). Noted for Chardonnay and late-harvest Johannisberg Riesling. Open daily for tastings and self-guided tours 10:00A.M.–4:30P.M.. **Sebastiani**, 389 4th Street, East

Sonoma (tel: (707) 938-5532). Good name for red wines; good tours. Open 10:00A.M.–5:00P.M..

In Livermore on East Bay, 48 miles (77km) from San Francisco, the majority of the residents are involved with nuclear research, but for visitors the area is of interest for its vineyards. The following wineries give tours and/or tastings.
Concannon Vineyard, 4590 Tesla Road (tel: 447-3760). Tastings Monday to Friday 10:00A.M.–4:30P.M., weekends from 11:00A.M.. Tours on weekends.
Elliston Vineyards, 483 Kilkare Road (tel: 862-2377). Tasting by appointment only.
Fenestra, 83 East Vallecitos Road (tel: 447-5246). Tastings on weekends noon–5:00P.M..
Livermore Valley Cellars, 1508

Wetmore Road (tel: 447-1751). Daily tasting 10:00A.M.–5:00P.M..
Wente Bros, 5565 Tesla Road (tel: 447-3603). Tastings Monday to Saturday 10:00A.M.–4:30P.M., Sunday 11:00A.M.–4:30P.M.. Tours Monday to Saturday 10:00A.M., 11:00A.M., 1:00, 2:00 and 3:00P.M.. Sunday at 1:00, 2:00, 3:00P.M..
Wente Bros Sparkling Wine Cellars, 5050 Arroya Road (tel: 447-3694). Tasting Monday to Saturday 10:00A.M.–5:00P.M., Sunday from 11:00A.M.. Tours on the hour 10:00A.M.–3:00P.M. (Sunday 1:00–3:00P.M.).
If this is not enough for you, *California is Wine Country*, a free guide to all the state's wineries and wine-growing regions, is available from the Wine Institute, 425 Market Street, Suite 1000, San Francisco 94105.

One of many Napa Valley wineries

SHOPPING

San Francisco is a mecca for the ardent shopper; in fact you will hardly know where to begin. The whole city is a world marketplace where you can find literally anything and everything, from whimsical novelties to excellent resort fashions. You will find splendid malls, department stores, specialty shops and trendy boutiques, as well as street stalls along the waterfront where local artisans sell their own handcrafted work.

The main downtown area is around Union Square, a busy but compact hub that is convenient and easy to get around. All the famous retail names are here (including a branch of Macy's), catering to every taste and budget, whether you are looking for knickknacks or designer sheets. In addition to the more elegant stores and well-known names there are some pleasant surprises and more unusual shops tucked away in offshoots like Maiden Lane. If you are a serious buyer, stick to the blocks bounded by Geary, Powell, Post and Stockton Streets.

The following shopping centers (even if you are just browsing) should not be missed.

American Indian Center, 225 Valencia Street (tel: 552-1070). A culturally based shopping center that focuses on food, art and entertainment in support of the American Indian.

The Anchorage, 2800 Leavenworth Street (tel: 775-6000). One-stop shopping in the heart of the Fisherman's Wharf area in a stylish complex of shops and restaurants and a

The Anchorage: waterfront shopping in the Fisherman's Wharf area

hotel. Designed to fit in with the seaport city scene, the complex is decorated with flags and banners and its outdoor promenades and decks offer several good viewing points over the bay. It covers one block, bounded by Jefferson, Leavenworth, Beach and Jones Streets – a 2.6-acre (1 hectare) site with its focal point, a two-story anchor sculpture, in Leavenworth Street Plaza. Street musicians and jugglers may be watched daily in the courtyard. There are over 50 boutiques selling gifts, prints, clothes,

SHOPPING

leather, jewelry and crafts. Can be reached by the Powell and Hyde cable cars or by bus (Nos 42 Sansome, 19 Polk, 30 Stockton and 32 Embarcadero all pass within a block of the Anchorage).

The Cannery, 2801 Leavenworth Street at Beach Street, between Fisherman's Wharf and Aquatic Park (tel: 771-3112). A favorite with visitors ever since it was transformed from Del Monte's 19th-century produce cannery into a glamorous three-storied complex of shops, art galleries, a toy museum, restaurants and cafés linked by arcades, bridges and balconies. From its balconies you can watch the bustle in the harbor and mimers and magicians perform in its courtyard. There are more than 50 specialty shops selling unusual foods and gifts, fine handcrafts and fashions. Best reached by the Hyde cable car to Aquatic Park and then a short walk.

Clement Street, Clement Street from Arguello Boulevard. An ethnic shopping district for a diverse range of goods from around the world. Many of the shops reflect the predominant nationalities of the area – Chinese, Jewish and Russian.

The Crocker Galleria, entrances on Post and Sutter Streets, between Montgomery and Kearny Streets (tel: 392-0100). Modeled after Milan's Galleria Vittorio Emmanuelle, this three-level pavilion under its glass dome is located near Union Square in the block bounded by Post, Kearny, Sutter and Montgomery Streets. There is a choice of some 50 specialty shops selling the best of American and European designer clothes and one-of-a-kind collectibles.

Embarcadero Center, between Sacramento, Market, Clay, Battery and Drumm Streets (tel: 772-0500). A site formerly occupied by San Francisco's produce market, this center is a boon to the financial district. It is almost a "city within a city," with its four office towers, the handsomely designed Hyatt Regency Hotel, its 375,000 square feet (35,000 sq m) of shopping and eating areas and its above-street pedestrian walkways. The Center frequently attracts impromptu entertainment and features major sculptures. Around 150 shops offering a variety of goods are

For upscale shopping, the Crocker Galleria offers cool elegance

found on three levels.

Ghirardelli Square, along the northern waterfront, bounded by North Point, Polk, Beach and Larkin Streets (tel: 775-5500). A much loved red-brick square block that once was a woollen mill and then a famous chocolate factory belonging to the Domingo Ghirardelli family. (Some of the original vats and ovens still operate at the Ghirardelli Chocolate Manufactory on the plaza level of the Clock Tower.) In the 1960s an innovative conversion turned this site into an attractive multilevel complex comprising 80 shops, galleries, outdoor cafés, restaurants and a theater, all overlooking the waterfront. A variety of free entertainment is often given in the West Plaza. Three bus lines (the 30 Stockton, the 42 Downtown Loop and the 19 Polk) run directly to Ghirardelli Square, while the Powell and Hyde cable cars bring you to within a block of the square.

Japan Center, bounded by Post, Geary, Laguna and Fillmore Streets (tel: 922-6776). You could almost be in Tokyo's Ginza in this three-square-block center. Decorated with fountains, an ornamental river and flowering plum and cherry trees, its five-acre (2 hectares) mall was designed by one of America's foremost architects, Minoru Yamasaki. As you might expect, the main features here are *sushi* bars and tea houses and shops selling oriental wares and foods. Reached by buses 2, 3, 4 or 38 (get off at Buchanan or Laguna Streets).

Pier 39, The Embarcadero (tel:

981-8030). A 45-acre (18-hectare) site that has been transformed from an old cargo pier into a waterfront marketplace. You will find over 100 shops and boutiques as well as restaurants on two levels lining the pier and a 350-berth marina beside it. Non-shoppers appreciate the family amusement area Funtasia, the old fashioned merry-go-round, the street performers and the San Francisco Experience (see page 106). From downtown take MUNI bus 15. Otherwise take 42 from Van Ness Avenue or the 32 from Market Street.

San Francisco Shopping Center, Market and Fifth Streets (tel: 495-5656). Opened in 1988, this nine-story vertical shopping mall's top five floors are a "store-in-the-sky." Eventually, more than 100 establishments with innovative "spiral" escalators will fill the building, selling California-style goods of all kinds.

At the concourse level of the Center there is an entrance to the Powell Street BART/MUNI station; a cable car "turn-around" is also conveniently located.

Union Street, Union Street between Russian Hill and the Presidio. Since the 1950s, merchants have been converting the old buildings into stylish boutiques, many of which sell antiques.

Upper Grant Avenue/North Beach, Grant Avenue between Columbus Avenue and Filbert Street. The place to hunt for the more unusual shops and restaurants in this area at the foot of Coit Tower.

ACCOMMODATIONS

It is no vain boast that San Francisco's accommodations run the full gamut from budget to luxury hotels.

At the top end you can expect to pay between $150 and $250 a single, but in the budget bracket single room rates start well under $50. In between there is a host of possibilities, including motor inns or lodge hotels and all suite hotels which, though they may not be cheap, give more space for your money. There are also a number of inns or so-called "boutique hotels" which often operate on a purely bed-and-breakfast basis, with perhaps sherry or tea in the later afternoon.

There are some things to remember about San Francisco hotels.

Almost everyone accepts credit cards but advance reservations are necessary, especially for the smaller B and B's.

A number of hotels do not charge for children sharing the same room as their parents, but each establishment decides individually on the age limit. (However, there are also many others which have large or connecting rooms priced with families in mind).

Room rates are subject to vast fluctuations but all rates are subject to what is called a Transient Occupancy Tax, at the time of writing 11 percent. Although the city is compact, various locations may be more suitable to your needs than others – this should be considered when comparing prices. Check-in time for guests in most hotels tends to be around 3:00P.M. (check-out by midday).

Luxury Hotels

Nob Hill
Fairmont Hotel and Tower, 950 Mason Street, top of Nob Hill (tel: 772-5000), offers 596 rooms and dignified service. A choice of seven restaurants includes a coffee shop, a 24-hour eatery and a supper club where top names can be found on the bill.
Mark Hopkins Inter-Continental, 1 Nob Hill (tel: 392-3434). If you are going to splurge, then why not do so on a hotel as celebrated as this one. It is, of course, superbly located with a notable cocktail lounge at its summit and all the necessary and extra facilities you would expect of an élite 391-room establishment. The views over the Bay are superlative and from the hotel it takes just minutes to reach Chinatown, Fisherman's Wharf or Union Square.
Stouffer Stanford Court, 905 California Street (tel: 989-3500). Also on Nob Hill is this traditional hotel with 402 rooms and a continental ambience.

On the Wharf
The Fisherman's Wharf area is another excellent accommodations base. Here, in the luxury bracket, the internationally known chain names such as Hyatt and Marriott are flourishing.
Hyatt Regency San Francisco, 5 Embarcadero Center (tel: 788-1234). Situated on the waterfront and a focal point for this business and shopping complex. There

The palatial Fairmont Hotel

are 803 rooms here and two of the cocktail lounges feature live music.

Mandarin Oriental, 222 Sansome Street (tel: 885-0999). The Embarcadero's other chic hotel, occupying the top 11 floors of the 48-story First Interstate Center. 160 rooms.

Park Hyatt San Francisco, 333 Battery Street (tel: 392-1234). A smaller and more exclusive Hyatt with 360 rooms.

San Francisco Marriott – Fisherman's Wharf, 1250 Columbus Avenue (tel: 775-7555). A good proportion of the 256 rooms have two double beds and there is a complimentary limousine service on weekdays to the financial district.

Sheraton at Fisherman's Wharf, 2500 Mason Street (tel: 362-5500). There are 525 rooms and a swimming pool in this waterfront location.

Union Square Area
The location with the largest amount of luxury accommodations is undoubtedly in the vicinity of Union Square in the heart of downtown San Francisco.

Four Seasons Clift, 495 Geary

ACCOMMODATIONS

Street (tel: 775-4700).
Personalized service is the
keynote here. There are 329
rooms, and extras include mini
bars and terry robes in the guest
rooms and "comp limo"
(complimentary limousine)
service to the financial district.
Grand Hyatt San Francisco, 345
Stockton Street (tel: 398-1234).
Offers the elegant service
associated with Hyatts
worldwide and has 693 rooms.
Hotel Nikko, 222 Mason Street
(tel: 394-1111). Has its own
health club/spa and 525 rooms.
Meridien, 50 Third Street (tel:
974-6400). A glamorous hotel
with 675 rooms.
Pan Pacific, 500 Post Street (tel:
771-8600). Personal care and
attention are emphasized at this
new 330-room hotel.
Park Fifty Five, 55 Cyril Magnin
Street (tel: 392-8000). Enormous
with 1,003 rooms, but a tiered
exterior allows maximum views.

*San Francisco's newest Marriott
hotel, downtown on Market Street*

Has its own fully equipped health
club.
**San Francisco Hilton on Hilton
Square**, 1 Hilton Square (tel:
771-1400). Another huge hotel
with 1,907 rooms, five
restaurants and a health club.
San Francisco Marriott, 55
Fourth Street (tel: 896-1600).
Forty storys dwarfing Yerba
Buena Gardens, 1,500 rooms.
Sheraton Palace, 2 New
Montgomery Street (tel: 392-
8600). Victorian styled in
everything except amenities,
550 rooms.
Sir Francis Drake, 450 Powell
Street (tel: 392-7755). One of the
city's best known hotels. There is
live music in the rooftop cocktail
lounge and a new Saks Fifth
Avenue next door. 417 rooms.
Westin St Francis, 335 Powell
Street (tel: 397-7000). Has been

a traditional choice for the discerning traveler since it opened in 1904. These days it has 1,200 rooms and five restaurants to its credit.

Moderate Hotels

Motels
In San Francisco motels offer one of the best bets in the moderate bracket when it comes to convenient location.
Air Travel Hotel, 655 Ellis Street (tel: 771-3000). Five blocks from the Civic Center. Has 100 rooms and free parking.
Howard Johnson's Motor Lodge, 580 Beach Street (tel: 775-3800). Situated at Fisherman's Wharf within easy walking distance of all attractions, yet easy on the pocket. 128 rooms and free guest parking.
Travelodge at Fisherman's Wharf, 250 Beach Street (tel: 392-6700). Has 250 rooms and its own swimming pool.
Travelodge at Ghirardelli Square, 1201 Columbus Avenue (tel: 776-7070). A tiny 25-room motel – really good value.
Travelodge Downtown, 790 Ellis Street (tel: 775-7612). Has 80 rooms and free parking.

Civic Center Area
First class accommodations in the vicinity of the Civic Center are quite plentiful. Best Western is one name to look for here.
Best Western Americania, 121 Seventh Street (tel: 626-0200). Offers free in-room films in its 142 guest units, free parking, a swimming pool, saunas and complimentary evening shuttle to Union Square – all for a

moderate price.
Best Western Carriage Inn, 140 Seventh Street (tel: 552-8600), is far smaller, only 48 rooms in Victorian style, but its rates include continental breakfast.
Best Western Civic Center Motor Inn, 364 Ninth Street (tel: 621-2826) has 57 rooms, free parking, free movies and a pool.
Best Western Flamingo Motor Inn, 114 Seventh Street (tel: 621-0701), offers good value for the money.
Holiday Inn – Civic Center, 50 Eighth Street (tel: 626-6103), has 390 rooms. One of several Holiday Inns in town.
Ramada Hotel San Francisco, 1231 Market Street (tel: 626-8000), is a landmark hotel in this district, now completely restored and offering accommodations in 460 rooms.

Union Square Area
The Union Square district has its fair share of well-rated hotels that do not break the bank.
Campton Place, 340 Stockton Street (tel: 781-5555), is more upscale and boasts a Europeanized service; 126 rooms.
Galleria Park, 191 Sutter Street (tel: 781-3060), goes back to 1911, but is updated enough to feature air-conditioning, sound-proofing, honor bars and a rooftop jogging track; 177 rooms.
Hotel Bedford, 761 Post Street (tel: 673-6040), is more continental-styled than some, with valet service and valet parking, 143 rooms and a four-star restaurant.
Hotel Californian, 405 Taylor Street (tel: 885-2500), 243 rooms, generally has an

ACCOMMODATIONS

international clientele despite its name.

Powell Hotel, 28 Cyril Magnin Street (tel: 398-3200). Another tastefully refurbished place, with 115 rooms.

Regis, 490 Geary Street (tel: 928-7900), was built in 1913 and restored to its original good looks in 1987. Its 86 rooms all feature marble bathrooms; some have canopied beds and some balconies.

Union Square, 114 Powell Street (tel: 397-3000). Comfortable rooms (131) and complimentary continental breakfast are assets here.

Villa Florence, 225 Powell Street (tel: 397-7700). Renovated to a good standard of comfort. Continental breakfast included in rates; 177 rooms.

Boutique Hotels

What is a "boutique" hotel? In some people's opinion it is a small, elegant, luxury class hotel offering personal service. In others, it is a small inn offering upscale bed and breakfast. The following recommendations are a combination.

Civic Center Area

Abigail, 246 McAllister Street (tel: 861-9728), is a 62-room Civic Center area hotel which strives to maintain an "English" inn warmth.

Phoenix Inn, 601 Eddy Street (tel: 776-1380), has 44 rooms and the assets of a swimming pool, sculpture garden, art gallery, all-day complimentary coffee, and nearby health club.

Union Square Area

There is more choice around Union Square.

Alamo Square Inn, 719 Scott Street (tel: 922-2055), should appeal to those with a penchant for 19th-century mansions. This one has 13 bedrooms, several of which have fireplaces. Rates here include complimentary breakfast.

Cartwright, 524 Sutter Street (tel: 421-2865). Each of the 114 rooms is furnished with antiques and fresh flowers. A home away from home that offers complimentary afternoon tea.

Donatello, 501 Post Street (tel: 441-7100), promises high standards of service. Offers 95 rooms and a well-regarded Italian restaurant as well as airport transportation.

Hotel David, 480 Geary Street (tel: 771-1600), is noted for its breakfasts. A quiet hideaway with 56 rooms.

Inn at The Opera, 333 Fulton Street (tel: 863-8400). "Custom designed" is the expression used by this luxurious little hotel located near the performing arts and government center. It has 48 queen-sized rooms with English furnishings.

Inn at Union Square, 440 Post Street (tel: 397-3510). Each floor has its own lobby and fireplace. No restaurant at this 30-room establishment but afternoon tea and evening hors d'oeuvres are offered and continental breakfast is complimentary.

Kensington Park, 450 Post Street (tel: 788-6400). Classically continental with 90 rooms.

King George, 334 Mason Street (tel: 781-5050). High tea is a specialty in this quiet and charming establishment. All the 143 rooms have been recently redecorated, and other

A bedroom in the King George Hotel, where the standard is quiet comfort

attractions are the Japanese restaurant and rooftop sundeck.

Monticello Inn, 127 Ellis Street (tel: 392-8800). Colonial style prevails at this 91-room hostelry.

Petite Auberge, 863 Bush Street (tel: 928-6000), French provincial style, though this 26-room B and B serves buffet breakfasts, courtesy afternoon tea, sherry and hors d'oeuvres.

Powell West, 111 Mason Street (tel: 771-1200). Reopened in 1988 as a handsomely appointed 55-room hostelry with its own restaurant/café.

Prescott, 545 Post Street (tel: 563-0303). With 167 rooms, this is that extra special place for discriminating tourists seeking a Union Square address, though

higher priced than some others in this category. Suites with a personal jacuzzi and signature restaurant are among the features.

Vintage Court, 650 Bush Street (tel: 392-4666). Overstuffed chairs but no stuffy ambience here. Complimentary tea, coffee and evening wine is served in the cozy lobby; 106 rooms.

White Swan Inn, 845 Bush Street (tel: 775-1755). A sophisticated but small 27-room hotel also in the heart of San Francisco, but with an English country inn atmosphere.

Other Locations

Annabella Victoria, 1801A Laguna Street (tel: 567-8972). Only five rooms and dating from 1884 with a Van Ness district address. Rates include breakfast.

Griffon, 155 Steuart Street (tel: 495-2100). A swimming pool and health club are among the amenities of this 62-roomed establishment at the Embarcadero.

Huntington, 1075 California Street (tel: 474-5400). At the peak of Nob Hill, this is the type of hotel that offers complimentary Rolls-Royce service daily to the downtown and business areas but includes a full breakfast selection in its rates; 140 rooms.

Majestic, 1500 Sutter Street (tel: 441-1100). In the Van Ness district, the 60-room hotel was built around 1902. It is grand and full of French Empire and English antiques.

Mansions, 2220 Sacramento Street (tel: 929-9444). Victorian styled with 28 rooms, piped-in classical music and complimentary breakfast; a unique bed and breakfast gem in Pacific Heights.

Nob Hill Inn, 1000 Pine Street (tel: 673-6080). Another gracious little hotel decorated in townhouse style, it is calm and genteel, with 21 rooms.

Queen Anne, 1590 Sutter Street (tel: 441-2828). A splendidly luxuriously Victorian 49-roomed guest house, formerly a girls' boarding school, which has won awards for its antique-filled accommodations in the Van Ness district.

Sherman House, 2160 Green Street (tel: 563-3600). Canopied feather beds and wood-burning fireplaces are the assets at this comfortable 15-room hotel in Pacific Heights.

Victorian Inn on the Park, 301 Lyon Street (tel: 931-1830). The décor captures the romance of the era in which it was built (1897).
A 12-room mansion in Golden Gate Park that includes continental breakfast in its rates.

Budget Hotels
Modestly priced, clean and comfortable hotels are scattered throughout the city. Among them, the following.

All Seasons, 417 Stockton Street (tel: 986-8737), with 90 rooms in a Union Square location.

Ansonia-Cambridge, 711 Post Street (tel: 673-2670). Easily affordable, with rates that include full breakfast and dinner; 130 rooms.

Beach Motel, 4211 Judah Street (tel: 681-6618). Offers 20 rooms at Ocean Beach.

Bel Air, 344 Jones Street (tel: 771-3460). Half the rooms have private bathrooms. Conveniently situated a block from the airport terminal.

Bentley Motor Inn, 465 Grove Street (tel: 864-4040). There is good value at this Civic Center location; 40 rooms.

Britton, 112 Seventh Street (tel: 621-7001). Renovated 1911 hotel with 79 rooms.

Broadway Manor, 2201 Van Ness Avenue (tel: 776-7900). A 60-room motor inn within easy reach of Fisherman's Wharf.

Budget Inn, 111 Page Street (tel: 626-4155). With 24 rooms in a Civic Center situation, it lives up to its name.

Cambridge, 473 Ellis Street (tel: 928-0905). Very much a tourist hotel with downtown shops in easy reach; 60 rooms.

Cornell, 715 Bush Street (tel: 421-3154). With 45 rooms and complimentary breakfast, this is a good buy between Nob Hill and Union Square. All rooms are non-smoking.

Embassy Motor Hotel, 610 Polk Street (tel: 673-1404). Near the Civic Center, it has 84 rooms, a Chinese restaurant and cocktail lounge.

Essex, 684 Ellis Street (tel: 474-4664). Has a more European atmosphere than some others – recently renovated.

Friendship Inn Civic Center, 860 Eddy Street (tel: 474-4374). Free guest parking. Jacuzzi or steam bath in some rooms.

Gates, 140 Ellis Street (tel: 781-0430). A short distance from Union Square, it offers rates you cannot fault; 66 rooms.

Geary, 610 Geary Street (tel: 673-9221). Good value in the Van Ness district; 92 rooms.

Grove Inn, 890 Grove Street (tel: 929-0780). A particularly nice Victorian bed and breakfast with 19 rooms. Alamo Square location.

Hotel One, 1087 Market Street (tel: 861-4946). This recently redecorated place really saves you money in the Civic Center locale; 174 rooms.

Hyde Plaza, 835 Hyde Street (tel: 885-2987). Though not all 51 rooms have *en suite* bathrooms, it is a good value.

Manor Motel/Friendship Inn, 2358 Lombard Street (tel: 922-2010). Reasonable, in the marina district.

Ocean Park Motel, 2690 46th Avenue (tel: 566-7020). An Art Deco motel across from the zoo.

Pensione International, 875 Post Street (tel: 775-3344). Basic but well maintained, near Union Square; 49 rooms.

San Remo, 2237 Mason Street (tel: 776-8688). A historic 62-room hotel a block from Fisherman's Wharf.

Sutter Larkin, 1048 Larkin Street (tel: 474-6820). Cheap rates but immaculate rooms may be found here; 34 rooms.

Temple, 469 Pine Street (tel: 781-2565). Cheap and clean, in the financial district.

Verona, 317 Leavenworth (tel: 771-4242), has been recently refurbished. Civic Center location; 65 rooms.

All-Suite Hotels

Americana Suites, 20 Franklin Street (tel: 553-8700), offers 75 suites, all with private bath and color TV in a central location at a modern price.

Art Center Bed and Breakfast, 1902 Filbert Street (tel: 567-1526). Offers five colonial-styled suites, an art studio and free breakfast, but no smokers please (except in back atrium). Ideal for those interested in art.

Classic Suites, 60 Leavenworth (tel: 626-3662). Each of the 24 suites has its own living room, dining area and fully equipped kitchen at reasonable rates.

Elles'Mere on Nob Hill, 655 Powell Street (tel: 477-4600). All 48 suites have full kitchens and stereo-TV entertainment centers. High-priced but some will think the Nob Hill location worth it.

Hyde Park Suites, 2655 Hyde Street (tel: 771-0200), near Fisherman's Wharf; 24 suites in the higher price bracket. Complimentary wine is served every evening in the atrium – so are pastries in the morning.

Nob Hill Suites, 955 Pine Street

ACCOMMODATIONS

(tel: 928-3131). Designed for the business traveler at good prices for a Nob Hill address.

Trinity Suites, 845 Pine Street (tel: 433-3330), features 18 elegant, Victorian-styled two-bedroom/two bathroom suites.

Chinatown/Japantown Locations

Some visitors might want specifically to base themselves in one of these locations.
In Chinatown you could try these.

Beverly Plaza, 342 Grant Avenue (tel: 781-3566). It could not be in a better spot at the heart of Chinatown and has 150 rooms in the medium price range.

Grant Plaza, 465 Grant Avenue (tel: 434-3883), boasts an equally good location and is in the budget bracket; 72 rooms.

Holiday Inn – Financial District, 750 Kearny Street (tel: 433-6600), just one block from Chinatown. Large and superior,

it has 566 rooms, modern amenities and superb views.

Royal Pacific Motor Inn, 661 Broadway (tel: 781-6661), midway between North Beach and Chinatown, is a moderately priced alternative with 74 rooms. Japantown can offer these.

Best Western Miyako Inn, 1800 Sutter Street (tel: 921-4000). A modern hotel in the heart of Japantown, about half of its 125 rooms have steam baths.

Miyako Hotel, 1625 Post Street (tel: 922-3200). There is Japanese décor with authentic Japanese furnishings in some suites; 218 rooms. Moderate prices.

Bed and Breakfast

Do not necessarily expect the offerings in this category to be cheap. Some, indeed, have been listed above under ''Boutique Hotels.''
Those not already mentioned include:

Best Western Kyoto Inn in Japantown, one of a chain but with Japanese touches to give it a more individual feel

ACCOMMODATIONS

Adelaide Inn, 5 Isadora Duncan Street, (tel: 441-2474). A quiet, European-style 16-room inn which is situated not far from Union Square that serves complimentary breakfast and has most modest rates.

Albion House Inn, 135 Gough Street (tel: 621-0896). Smaller than the Adelaide (eight rooms), more elegant, more expensive, and located near the Opera House. Built in 1906, it boasts antique furnishings and a piano in the parlor.

Golden Gate, 775 Bush Street (tel: 392-3702). Most of the 25 rooms have *en suite* bathrooms, and antique furnishings add to a cozy atmosphere.

Inn on Castro, 321 Castro Street (tel: 861-0321). This inn has only five rooms but offers plenty of continental breakfast for those with a hearty appetite. Inexpensive.

Red Victorian, 1665 Haight Street (tel: 864-1978), is decorated in 1960s style and has 15 rooms.

Spencer House, 1080 Haight Street (tel: 626-9205), is furnished with antiques and serves its guests a full breakfast. Relatively expensive.

Union Street Inn, 2229 Union Street (tel: 346-0424). An Edwardian-styled guest house that serves continental breakfast in the parlor or the English garden. On the small side with only six rooms.

Washington Square Inn, 1660 Stockton Street (tel: 981-4220), is quiet and comfortable, in the medium price range. Situated in the North Beach location with 15 rooms.

A list of B and B accommodations may be obtained from Bed and Breakfast International – San Francisco, 1181-B Solano Avenue, Albany, 94706 (tel: 525-4569).

Apartments

Some visitors prefer the freedom and independence of a furnished apartment. The following companies can assist with short-term accommodations in all price ranges in apartments.

American Property Exchange, 170 Page Street, San Francisco 94102 (tel: 863-8484).

At Home, 5635 Sunfish Court, Byron 94514 (tel: 757-5536).

Commercial Services, 28 North First Street, San José 95113 (tel: (408) 279-3747).

Executive Suites, 840 Post Street, San Francisco 94109 (tel: 567-5151).

Grosvenor House Apartments, 899 Pine Street, San Francisco 94108 (tel: 421-1899).

Hillpoint Guest Houses and Apartments, 15 Hillpoint Avenue, San Francisco 94117 (tel: 753-0393).

Hotel Alternative, 1125 East Hillsdale Boulevard, Suite 105, Foster City 94404 (tel: 578-1366).

Northpoint Apartments, 2211 Stockton Street, San Francisco 94133 (tel: 989-6563).

Post Street Towers, 737 Post Street, San Francisco 94109 (tel: 771-7784).

St Francis Play, One St Francis Place, San Francisco 94107 (tel: 777-1512).

Vacation Rentals, P.O.B. 4426, Salinas 93902 (tel: (408) 757-7883).

Guest Houses/Hostels (see **Tight Budget**, page 106)

NIGHTLIFE AND ENTERTAINMENT

There is no shortage of nightlife in San Francisco, which always has something to suit all tastes. A bawdy past may account for the sidewalk sellers and strip joints (most prevalent in North Beach along the Broadway nightlife belt), but equally it has been a cultural city from its earliest beginnings, offering superb opera, ballet and music. Many of the sleazier places are in reality tamer than you might think and the plusher places are really glitzy. Lots of the cafés offer live music – guitar perhaps – and dance and jazz clubs are scattered throughout the neighborhoods. San Francisco has a hefty gay population and a number of bars and clubs are designated "gay," although not necessarily to the exclusion of anyone else.

For how to find out what's going on in town, see **Directory**, page 120–1.

Tickets

Tickets for all types of events, including sports and theater, may be purchased from Ticketron, whose downtown box office is at 325 Mason Street (call 392-SHOW to make a credit card booking or 546-9400 for information). Performing Arts Services (STBS), Stockton Street between Geary and Post Streets on the east side of Union Square, also at One Embarcadero Center, sells half-price tickets on the day of performance for all types of arts events (call 433-STBS for recorded information). It also sells full-price tickets in advance for almost all major attractions. To obtain a half-price ticket, you must show up in person (Tuesday to Saturday noon–7:30P.M.; or at Embarcadero Center, Monday to Friday 10:00A.M.–6:00P.M.). Pay in cash.

Where to Go

Concerts, Ballet and Opera

The city maintains an excellent symphony orchestra (the San Francisco Symphony) at the Davies Symphony Hall in the Civic Center. The Subscription Season (September to May) is virtually always sold out but tickets are usually available for the non-subscription programs, such as Merrill Lynch Great Performers Series (September to May); New and Unusual Music (October to May); Mozart Festival (June); Joffrey Ballet at the War Memorial Opera House (July); POPS Concerts in the Civic Auditorium (July) and some other special events. All tickets and information can be obtained at the Symphony Box Office (tel: 431-5400).

Today's Artists Concerts have been running a first-class series of recitals and chamber concerts for many years now during the season (September to April). Performances are scheduled at a variety of times either at the Masonic Auditorium or the Herbst Theater. Call 398-1324 for information.

The **Midsummer Music Festival** (mid-June to mid-August) is held in Sigmund Stern Memorial Grove. There are 10 Sunday afternoon programs at 2:00P.M. featuring all types of

Strip clubs on Broadway, the sleazier aspect of San Francisco's nightlife

music and dance for free. Call 398-6551 for information. Free Sunday orchestral and band concerts take place all year in Golden Gate Park.

The **San Francisco Ballet** is not only highly regarded in California but is one of the US's principal companies. During the repertory season (late January to early May), classical ballets and new work are presented at the War Memorial Opera House. During the Christmas holidays, several performances of *Nutcracker Suite* are spectacularly staged. Tickets and information are available from the Ballet Box Office or by calling 861-1177. **San Francisco Opera** is one of the leading opera companies with a 13-week long season (September to December). Grand Opera featuring internationally acclaimed artists is presented in repertory in the Opera House. Tickets are available at the

Opera Box Office (10:00A.M.–6:00P.M., except Sunday) or call 864-3330.

Theater
Classics and the best of Broadway take to the stage at the **Geary Theater**, 415 Geary Street (tel: 673-6440), where San Francisco's award-winning repertory company (the American Conservatory Theater) stages full-scale professional productions in season (late October to May) and special attractions in summer.

Centrally located in the Civic Center, the **Zephyr Theater**, 25 Van Ness Avenue (tel: 861-6655), has an ongoing production schedule throughout the year in all three of its theaters.

Broadway-style plays and musicals are presented at the **Curran Theater**, 445 Geary Street (tel: 474-3800); the **Golden Gate Theater**, 25 Taylor Street (tel: 474-3800); and the **Orpheum Theater**,

NIGHTLIFE AND ENTERTAINMENT

Bars and nightclubs catering to all tastes abound in the bright lights of San Francisco

1192 Market Street (tel: 474-3800).

The **Magic Theater** is the city's second largest resident theater, located in Fort Mason Center (tel: 441-8822). In addition to a five-play season there is a six-week Spring Festival featuring new plays plus a Performing Arts series.

A full range of dramas, comedies and musicals are staged in the Kensington Park Hotel's new 700-seat **Theater on the Square**, 450 Post Street (tel: 433-9500).

At the **Lorraine Hansberry Theater**, 620 Sutter Street (tel: 474-8800), a black theater company offers stage entertainment all year.

Cinema

The city has over 50 cinemas, most of which can be found on Geary Boulevard, Clement Street, Union Street, Fillmore Street and Van Ness Avenue.

The **Pacific Film Archive**, at 2625 Durant Avenue (call 642-1124 for recorded schedule information), shows some of the best old and modern films at economy rates, plus some showings from the San Francisco International Film Festival held from April to May each year. For a program call: 931-FILM.

Cabaret/Musical Revues

One of the most famous and established nightclubs which has featured female impersonators (all in good taste) for 50 years is **Finocchio's**, 506 Broadway (tel: 982-9388). There are three lavish shows nightly at 8:30P.M. except Monday and Wednesday.

Beach Blanket Babylon is a cabaret-style show (it has been going for 17 years and tickets are still in great demand) at the **Club Fugazi**, 678 Green Street, North Beach (tel: 421-4222). Show time is Wednesday and Thursday at 8:00P.M., Friday and Saturday at 8:00 and 10:30P.M. and Sunday at 3:00P.M. (this afternoon spot is the one time under-21s are welcome and only soft drinks are sold) and 7:30P.M..

Premier cabaret is staged in the York Hotel's **Plush Room**, 940 Sutter Street. For a program call 885-2800.

If you are looking for a first-class comedy club, the **Punch Line**, 444A Battery Street (tel: 397-7573), is where you are likely to see both local and nationally known comedians. The club is normally open from Sunday to Thursday at 9:00P.M., Friday and

Saturday performances at 9:00 and 11:00P.M..

Top entertainers often play what is now the West Coast's largest nightclub, the **Warfield Theater**, 982 Market Street (tel: 775-7722). Star turns are on Thursday (9:00P.M.–3:00A.M.) and on Friday and Saturday (9:00P.M.–4:00A.M.).

New competition for Finocchio's is the rollicking female impersonator cabaret put on twice nightly and enjoyed by all (8:00 and 9:30P.M.) Wednesday to Sunday at **Puttin' on the Glitz**, 571 Mission Street (tel: 541-0633).

Jazz, Folk and Rock

The best areas for intimate jazz and folk music clubs are the North Beach–Upper Grant Avenue district and that known as SoMa (south of Market Street).

Some of the best country, rock, jazz and folk music may be heard at the **Great American Music Hall**, 859 O'Farrell Street (tel: 885-0750), which also serves dinner until 11:30P.M..

For bluesy-type music try **Slim's**, 333 Eleventh Street (tel: 621-3330), a 300-seat nightclub with a Californian-cuisine restaurant (open Tuesday to Sunday 8:00P.M.–2:00A.M.).

Dancing

One of the most elegant places to dance the evening away is the **Starlite Roof** of the Sir Francis Drake Hotel, Sutter and Powell Streets (tel: 392-7755), where the city views from the 21st floor are impressive. Open nightly until 12:30A.M. (to 1:00A.M. Friday and Saturday).

In the **New Orleans Room** of the Fairmont Hotel, 950 Mason Street (tel: 772-5259), music from the swing era predominates nightly until around 1:00A.M.. Teatime music to sway to is good in the **Atrium Lobby** of the Hyatt Regency, 5 Embarcadero Center (tel: 788-1234), and in the grand bar of the Westin St Francis, Union Square (tel: 774-0167).

Sound, light and a 12-foot (3.5m) video screen heighten the vibrations that go on all night at **The Palladium**, 1031 Kearny Street at Broadway (tel: 434-1308). The latest hits to dance the night away to are played on three floors Thursday to Sunday from 9:00P.M.–6:00A.M..

Pop, rock, rhythm, blues – everything that's "hot" – is played in the **Cisco Kid Cantina** at the base of the Transamerica Pyramid, 600 Montgomery Street (tel: 983-4800). It is open until 4:00A.M. on Friday and Saturday nights.

Nightly dancing plus live entertainment can be found at **Club DV8** in the SoMa nightlife quarter, 55 Natoma Street (tel: 777-1419), open from 9:00P.M. to 2:00A.M. Wednesday, 3:00A.M. Thursday and 4:00A.M. Friday and Saturday.

Hotspot for the energetic and young is **Soiree Dance Club**, 3231 Fillmore Street at Lombard (tel: 567-4004).

DJs spin tunes from the 1950s and 1960s at **Rockin' Robins**, 1840 Haight Street (tel: 221-1960), open nightly to 2:00A.M., and you will find both DJs and live bands at **The Oasis**, 278 11th Street at Folsom (tel: 621-

8119), also open until 2:00A.M..
An upscale atmosphere is what
you will find in **Oz** at the Westin
St Francis Hotel, Union Square
(tel: 397-7000).

If you like sports as much as
you like moving to music,
Houlihan's Old Place at The
Anchorage, 2800 Leavenworth
Street (tel: 775-7523), has one
of the answers – big screen
football and baseball on
Monday night. Super screens,
too, at the **Jukebox Saturday
Night**, 650 Howard Street (tel:
495-JUKE), which shows sports
teams in action while sounds of
the 1950s and 1960s play. And
at **Rock and Bowl**, 1855 Haight
Street (tel: 826-BOWL), that is
exactly what you do – dance
and bowl!

WEATHER AND WHEN TO GO

Some people make the mistake
of thinking San Francisco has
the weather of southern
California. Although it can boast
a temperate marine climate
year round, it is not the place
for skimpy and exotic resort
wear. Summer temperatures,
for instance, rarely rise above
70°F (21°C), so you should
never feel too hot or sticky.
Winter temperatures rarely fall
below 41°F (5°C), and that
means that you will never be
terribly cold here. San
Francisco gets its share of rain,
most of it falling in the winter
months (November to March),
and certainly morning mist,
most common during the
summer months though
generally it does not persist into
the day.

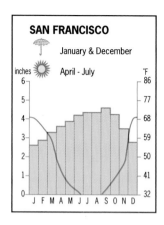

What to Wear

Since the climate is mild all year,
neither very lightweight nor very
heavyweight clothing is practical.
Suits and slacks, sportswear and
attire that comes with a jacket
are eminently suitable for both
men and women. Layered
clothing – blouses or shirts with
pullovers, sweaters or
cardigans – is recommended,
along with an all-weather or rain
coat, umbrella and comfortable
walking shoes for getting up and
down those hills and around the
islands.

When to Go

With boating and beaches in
mind, summer is the answer,
but every time of year is a
good time for San Francisco if
you are not into sunbathing. The
city is always packed with
visitors, but most especially in
summer when school is out. In
autumn, Napa Valley's wine
country is extraordinarily
popular with both locals and
vacationers, so don't expect to

have the wineries to yourself.

HOW TO BE A LOCAL

Be laid back and let the world go by and you are almost a native. Yet there is a touch of *haute couture* class to all this casualness and certain rules still apply – never wear an aloha shirt (that is the bright floral kind) to the opening of the opera season, which is a Gala in the grand tradition. And if you would rather not risk being beaten over the head, *don't* refer to "The Mark" (as in the hotel) as "The Hopkins," and very definitely *don't* refer to the city as "Frisco."

Other than that, by being a tourist, you are as good as local. They all use their feet a lot for getting around and have a love affair with their cable cars. They all eat seafood as much as possible and love fresh salads whether or not it is December.

Locals love the city's cable car system just as much as visitors

But they do know that the sign that says "grade" or "hill" really does mean "steep," and they will never be found swimming in San Francisco Bay – it is *far* too cold. Although local San Franciscans tend to act and dress casually for the most part, they like to be chic and are always up-to-date with the latest fashion trends. Indeed, they often set them! That is why so many fads, trends and gimmicks make their début in this Californian city, so if you want to fit in do not be stuffy but go for the novelty factor.

There may have been prejudice in the past but that past is over. Nowadays, feeling at home in San Francisco means being comfortable and mixing with a widely diverse section of people of all kinds of ethnic origins and inclinations. Providing you do not actually break the law, the locals are quite tolerant.

PERSONAL PRIORITIES

It is well known that San Francisco has a large gay population. However, if you are not gay you will certainly not feel out of place. If you are gay or lesbian you should know that many of the city's gay bars and gay-owned businesses and restaurants are located around Polk and Geary Streets, Pacific Avenue and Castro Street, south of Market Street to 19th Street where much of the gay and lesbian population lives. However, gay nightlife is certainly not confined to these areas. When seeking nightlife, you should be able to tell which bars and clubs cater to a gay clientele.

Safety

It should be borne in mind that some areas such as Mission District are popular with street criminals who target visitors. For safety's sake it is advisable not to wander into the area known as the Western Addition, a section bounded by Gough Street to the east, Masonic Avenue to the west, Geary Boulevard to the north and Duboce Avenue to the south. Avoid the Tenderloin district at night too, a triangle bounded by Ellis Street to the north, Market Street to the south and east and Hyde Street to the west.

Emergency Needs

San Francisco is one of the most cosmopolitan and civilized cities in the world, and there is next to nothing which cannot be bought there.

Local pharmacies will carry almost any personal item you might need.

CHILDREN

San Francisco is such a fun city that it will appeal as much to youngsters as to their parents. Something is always going on at the popular shopping centers, for instance. Kids may be bored by browsing around stores, but they will enjoy the free street entertainment – the jugglers, mime artists, magicians – who find their way to complexes like The Anchorage and Embarcadero Center, while Pier 39 has its own family entertainment area (see

The merry-go-round is just one attraction to keep the children happy on Pier 39

Shopping, page 85).
Eating out with children is no
problem in San Francisco. They
are not only welcome in
restaurants but are often provided
with something to occupy them
(crayons and drawings to color)
while waiting for food.
What with beaches on the
doorstep and boat trips in the
Bay, outdoor enjoyment is easy –
and all ages want to ride a cable
car. There are bridges to cross
and hills and buildings to climb
for fantastic views and plenty of
park space with areas specially
designated for children. For
information about playgrounds,
call the San Francisco Recreation
and Parks Department at 558-
3706.

Fun and Theme Parks
Children's Fairyland, Grand
Avenue and Bellevue entrance to
Lakeside Park. Geared to small
fries – no adults without a child.
Open: summer 10:00A.M. to
4:00P.M. (weekends until 5:00P.M.);
rest of the year 10:00A.M.–4:30P.M..
Golden Gate Park, McLaren
Lodge (Fell and Stanyon Streets).
There are acres and acres to this
recreation area which also
contains the **California
Academy of Sciences**. One
component of the latter is the
Steinhart Aquarium, a particularly
large and diverse collection of
aquatic life. Among the
"residents" are several penguins;
watch them line up for their chow
every day at 11:30A.M. and
2:00P.M.. And in Fish Roundabout
(a vast circular tank) there are
sharks and ocean fish. Small
children usually head for the
Touching Tidepool where they
can examine a hermit crab or

starfish at close quarters. Slightly
older visitors might enjoy the
Earth and Space Hall where they
can ride the Safe Quake and
experience what it is like being
in an earthquake. There is also
the Morrison Planetarium where
daily sky shows are given and,
on certain evenings, rock music
and light shows. There is an
additional charge for
planetarium shows. Call 750-
7141 for prices and schedules.
Academy open: 10:00A.M.–5:00P.M.
(later in summer). Admission
charge except for the under-sixes
and on the first Wednesday of
the month. Also located in Golden
Gate Park is a special children's
playground whose highlight is a
1912 merry-go-round.
Great America, South Bay, Santa
Clara (about 45 miles/72km
south of the city on US101 to
Great America Parkway). A
theme park with something for
all the family on a 100-acre/40-
hectare site. There are five
themed areas: Hometown
Square, Yukon Territory, Yankee
Harbor, County Fair and Orleans
Place. Naturally, the thrill rides
here are the big attraction:
youngsters can take the Rip
Roaring Rapids white-water raft
ride or a spin in one of the
dizzying roller coasters. Those
too afraid or too young to have
their stomach churned can opt
for tamer rides like Fort Fun and
Smurf Woods. A variety of stage
shows are presented in five
theaters and there are also
dolphins and a giant-screen movie.
No shortage of places to eat.
Open: Easter week and daily in
summer; weekends only in
spring and autumn (closed
November to early March).

CHILDREN

Open from 10:00A.M. – closing time varies. Admission charge except for little ones under two. For 24-hour recorded information call (408) 988-1800.

Haunted Gold Mine, 117 Jefferson Street. A place of fantasy using illusion techniques. *Open*: daily 9:00A.M.–10:00P.M. (except Friday and Saturday until midnight in summer). Admission charge.

Raging Waters, 2333 South White Road, San José (about 55 minutes' drive south of San Francisco, off Capitol Expressway at Tully Road). A water-themed amusement park that features over 35 attractions, among them several thrill slides, river rides and activity pools. *Open*: daily 10:00A.M.–7:00P.M. mid-June to early September (late September, weekends only, weather permitting). Admission charge but under-fours free. For information call (408) 238-9900.

Santa Cruz Beach Boardwalk, 400 Beach Street, Santa Cruz (74 miles/119kms south of San Francisco, via US1). The only amusement park by a beach. Features a 1911 merry-go-round and a 1924 Giant Dipper roller coaster, vintage classics. There are other rides, too, plus game arcades and an indoor miniature golf course. *Open*: daily from 11:00A.M. in summer; weekends and holidays only in spring and autumn. Entrance is free but a fixed price pays for unlimited rides. For recorded information call (408) 426-7433.

Zoos and Wildlife Parks
Marine World/Africa USA, Marine World Parkway, Vallejo (about 30 miles/48km northeast of the city), also reached by catamaran from Pier 41, Fisherman's Wharf. Showcases all types of animals both in "starring" roles and in innovative habitats. The major presentations focus on killer whales, dolphins, sea lions, tigers, elephants, chimpanzees and exotic birds and butterflies. There are also humans in a first-class troupe of water-skiers. Elephant and camel rides are offered and one of the unique elements of Marine World is meeting animals with their trainers as they roam through the park. For young children there are animal encounter areas in the Gentle Jungle or they can learn more about animal life in the Chevron Learning Center. Additionally, the energetic (under-13s) can let off steam in the Whale-of-a-Time World, a playground inside a lifesize Blue Whale model. *Open*: daily 9:30A.M.–6:30P.M. in summer, Wednesday to Sunday 9:30A.M.–5:30P.M. the rest of the year. Admission charge but children under four free. For information call (707) 644-4000.

Monterey Bay Aquarium, 886 Cannery Row, Monterey (133 miles/214km south of the city via US 101). Destination for a day's outing or overnight excursion, this aquarium houses more than 6,500 creatures which can be seen in habitat galleries and exhibit areas. In the 90-foot (27.5m) Monterey Bay habitats, for example, you can watch sharks and ocean fish flash by, while California sea otters frolic happily in their own two-story habitat.

Open: daily 9:30A.M.–6:00P.M. in summer (from 10:00A.M. rest of year). Admission charge, but under-threes free. For information call (408) 648-4888.
San Francisco Zoo, on Sloat Boulevard with entrance at 45th Avenue. One of America's top six city zoos, this one is a masterpiece of design and uses computer technology and participatory techniques to tell the animals' stories. One of the most sophisticated exhibits is the Primate Discovery Center. Here the Nocturnal Gallery creates a midnight world for exotic nocturnal primates. Another favorite is Gorilla World, a split-level domain, carpeted in African grass, with eight viewing areas. Or there is the wolves' lair, a naturalistic environment known as Wolf Woods. The more unusual denizens of this zoo include koalas, snow leopards, white rhino and pigmy hippos; for the children there is a special petting zoo where they can feed young animals, and an Insect Zoo.
Open: daily all year 10:00A.M. to 5:00P.M. (Children's Zoo 11:00A.M.–4:00P.M., weather permitting). Admission charge but accompanied children under 12 free, also free to all first Wednesday of each month. For information call 753-7083.

Museums
American Carousel Museum, 633 Beach Street. Everyone loves a carousel and this museum displays the best examples of old fashioned carved animals for merry-go-rounds built between 1880 and 1930. (Exhibits change quarterly). Besides familiar handcarved horses, other figures include a lion, tiger, giraffe and rabbit; there are also slides and photos, and an authentic Wurlitzer band organ provides traditional carnival music. Workshop demonstrations are also given on restoration techniques. (The Museum will be closed until May 1994. Call for further details before your visit.) For information call 928-0550.
Balclutha, Pier 43, Fisherman's Wharf. A component of the Maritime National Historic Park, this square-rigged sailing vessel was built in 1886 and may be boarded.
Open: daily 10:00A.M.–6:00P.M. (until 5:00P.M. in winter). Admission charge but accompanied children under 17 free.
Exploratorium, Palace of Fine Arts, 3601 Lyon Street at Marina Boulevard. Very much a hands-on experience, with some 700 exhibits that are meant to be manipulated or activated with a press of a button., They are all concerned with science and human perception, from Einstein's Theory of Relativity to optics and audiology, and are designed to heighten awareness. Guaranteed to keep children fully occupied.
Open: 10:00A.M.-9:30P.M. Wednesday, 10:00A.M.–5:00P.M. Thursday to Sunday. Admission to Tactile Gallery includes general museum entrance charge and under-sixes free. Free to all the first Wednesday of the month and every Wednesday after 6:00P.M.. For information call 563-7337.
Guiness Museum of World Records, 235 Jefferson Street, Fisherman's Wharf. The place to

find out the most amazing things by means of print, artifacts and re-enactments or by video footage of records being set. Hands-on exhibits, too.
Open: daily 9:00A.M.–11:00P.M. (10:00A.M.–10:00P.M. in winter, except Friday and Saturday when open until midnight). Admission charge (under-fours free). For information call 771-9890.

International Toy Museum, 2801 Leavenworth, The Cannery, Fisherman's Wharf. A collection of dolls, trains and other toys from bygone eras plus a play space with new toys for children to try out.
Open: Tuesday to Saturday 10:30A.M.–5:00P.M., Sunday 11:00A.M.–5:00P.M.. Admission charge but under-twos free. For information call 861-8000.

Ripley's Believe It or Not!, 175 Jefferson Street. A museum that contains the odd, the unusual, the unique. There are more than 200 exhibits in 12 galleries, including a shrunken human torso and a cable car made from over 275,000 matchsticks. And all the facts are true.
Open: 10:00A.M.–10:00P.M. (until midnight Friday and Saturday). Admission charge (under-fives free). For information call 771-6188.

The San Francisco Experience, Pier 39, Fisherman's Wharf. Not exactly a museum but a good, and entertaining, introduction to the city by way of a wide-screen, multimedia show that tells San Francisco's story.
Thanks to special effects, the great 1906 earthquake and fire are recreated before your eyes and, whatever the time of year,

you can be part of the annual Chinese New Year Celebration. The presentation is equally informative, telling you how the bridges were built and how the cable cars run.
Open: daily 10:00A.M.–10:00P.M. with presentations every half hour. Admission charge but under-sixes free. For information call 982-7550.

Winner's Circle Ranch, 5911 Lakeville Highway, Petaluma (a 40-minute drive from the city, off US101). Miniature horses only 34 inches (86cm) high and under perform here. Shows are both entertaining and educational; the tiny horses include the world's smallest stallion.
Open: Wednesday to Sunday, 1 May to Labor Day (September), 10:30A.M.–4:00P.M. with shows at 11:00A.M. and 2:00P.M.. Admission charge. For information call (707) 762-0220.

TIGHT BUDGET

Somewhere to Stay

Considering that San Francisco is so popular with foreigners and other Americans, it is surprising how far a small budget can go. the central branch of the **YMCA**, 220 Golden Gate Avenue (tel: 885-0460), might well be the accommodation answer (it has 104 rooms, pool, sauna, gym and running track). Rooms are modest, but comfortable.
But there are other hostelries that are just as cheap and sometimes cheaper if you are prepared to look around.

Youth Hostale Centrale, for example, at 116 Turk Street (tel: 346-7835), is clean and very inexpensive if you do not mind sharing a room, and still a bargain if you reserve one to yourself. Many students opt for the **El Capitan Hotel** in the Mission District at 2361 Mission Street (tel: 695-1597), where 17 of the 23 rooms have private baths and weekly rates are available.

The **European Guest House**, 761 Minna Street (tel: 861-6634), around the Civic Center, costs peanuts but you will be sharing dormitory style. Young international travelers frequently find the **Interclub/Globe Hostel**, 10 Hallam Place (tel: 431-0540), suits them. It is south of Market Street and all its 30 rooms have *en suite* bathrooms.

One block from the airline terminal, the **Olympic**, 140 Mason Street (tel: 982-5010), is a sure bet for the slim wallet, or you could use the residence hall of the **San Francisco State University**, 800 Font Boulevard (tel: 338-2721), during summer months and year round at the University's Guest Center. For other recommended budget hotels, see **Accommodations**, page 92–3.

Cheap Eating

When it comes to eating out, frankly there are so many fast food outlets, bakeries, crêperies, salad bars and delis that it should not prove difficult to get fed. Of course you will see **MacDonald's**, as well as **Taco Bell**, **Jack in the Box** and **Carl's Jr** chains. Then there are the ice-cream shops like **Double Rainbow** (in several locations), **Just Desserts** and **J Higby's Yogurt Shoppes**.

Chinatown and Japantown are naturally good bets for less pricey fare, but there are no one area or one type of cuisine that ensures you do not part with too much cash. Among the established inexpensive places to check are the **Eagle Café** at

Good, cheap cafés like Red's near Pier 28, are not hard to find and kind to your budget

TIGHT BUDGET

Pier 39, which has been a waterfront favorite for ages, for hamburgers and the like. The **Golden Dragon** on Chinatown's Washington Street certainly costs less than some of its neighbors and *dim sum* at the **Hang Ah Tea Room** on Chinatown's street of the same name, at No 1, should be a filling experience.
Houlihan's Old Place at The Anchorage, Fisherman's Wharf is a name that has been around for years, satisfying palate and pocket. **Pepe's**, at Pier 39, since it serves Mexican cuisine can be guaranteed to satisfy the stomach rather inexpensively. And who can resist deep dish pizza – **Pizzeria Uno** on Powell Street (2323) at Fisherman's Wharf, or their other outlet on Lombard Street (2200), are worth a try. If you want to sit down to eat seafood rather than walking the waterfront with a carton, try **Rusty Scupper** at 1800 Montgomery Street at the Embarcadero. A good self-service place for soups and salads is **Salmagundi** on Market Street, Civic Center and at downtown Geary Street or the Embarcadero Center. Straightforward local (non-ethnic) fare is available at **Sears Fine Foods** on Powell Street around Union Square. For details of these and other cheap eating places, see also **Food and Drink**, page 79.

Entertainment on the Cheap

Impromptu street entertainment – which happens everywhere in San Francisco but particularly around the waterfront shopping complexes – is always free. To see cultural events, such as theater, you can save money by dropping in at the STBS ticket office on the Stockton Street side of Union Square, or at One Embarcadero Center, or receiving recorded information from them by dialing 433-STBS. Patterned after New York's TKTS, STBS sells half-price tickets on the day of performance for many attractions throughout the Bay area, It is cash only and you must present yourself in person. Tuesday to Saturday between noon and 7:30P.M.. Free band concerts, by the way, are often given on Sundays (all year round) in Golden Gate Park. There are quite a few museums and other places of interest to which entrance is free, and others which are free at certain times. Such attractions (at the time of writing) follow.

Asian Art Museum in Golden Gate Park, first Wednesday of every month and Saturdays 10:00A.M.–noon.
A World of Oil (Chevron USA's exhibit) on Market Street.
Cable Car Museum on Nob Hill.
California Academy of Sciences in Golden Gate Park, first Wednesday of every month.
California Historical Society, Whittier Mansion, on Jackson Street, first Wednesday of every month.
California Palace of the Legion of Honor in Lincoln Park, first Wednesday of every month and Saturdays 10:00A.M.–noon.
Chinese Culture Center at the Holiday Inn on Kearny Street.
Chinese Historical Society of America on Commercial Street.
Exploratorium at the Marina, first Wednesday of every month and Wednesday evenings

TIGHT BUDGET/SPECIAL EVENTS

6:00–9:30P.M..
Fort Point National Historic Site
at the Presidio.
Japanese Tea Garden in Golden
Gate Park, first Wednesday of
every month.
**Joseph Dee Museum of
Photography** on Kearny Street.
Kong Chow Temple on Stockton
Street (free – donations).
Mexican Museum at Fort Mason,
first Wednesday of every month.
**M H de Young Memorial
Museum** in Golden Gate Park,
first Wednesday of every month
and Saturdays 10:00A.M.–noon.
Mission Dolores (free, though a
donation is suggested).
Museo Italo Americano at Fort
Mason.
**Museum of Money of the
American West** (a Bank of
California exhibit) on California
Street.
North Beach Museum on
Stockton Street.
Old US Mint at 5th and Mission
Streets.
Presidio Army Museum on
Lincoln Boulevard.
**San Francisco Fire Department
Museum**, Presidio Avenue at
Pine Street.
**San Francisco History Room
and Archives** at the Civic
Center.
**San Francisco Museum of
Modern Art** at the Civic Center,
first Tuesday of every month,
while Thursdays 5:00P.M.–
9:00P.M. half-price.
San Francisco Zoo is free one
day in the month, days vary.
Society of California Pioneers
on McAllister Street.
Strybing Arboretum in Golden
Gate Park.
Wells Fargo History Museum
on Montgomery Street.

For more information on many of
these see **What to See**, page 12.

SPECIAL EVENTS

Dates and sites of events are
subject to change so do check
whenever possible.

January
Concerts in the Masonic
Auditorium and Herbst Theater.
San Francisco Sports and Boat
Show, Cow Palace.
International Boat Show,
Moscone Center or Cow Palace.
Shrine East-West All Star
Football Classic and Pageant,
Stanford Stadium, Palo Alto.
Martin Luther King Birthday
Celebration, Civic Auditorium.
Mozart Festival, Davies Hall.
Ballet season, Opera House.

February
Chinese New Year Celebration
and Parade in Chinatown (late
January to early February).

March
Tulipmania, Pier 39.
San Francisco Chronicle Great
Outdoor Adventure Fair,
Concourse Exhibition Center.
National Championship Cat
Show, Cow Palace.
St Patrick's Day Parade (Sunday
nearest 17 March).
Macy's Easter Flower Show,
Stockton and O'Farrell Streets.
Bach Birthday Program, Davies
Hall.
Cherry Blossom time at the
Japanese Tea Garden in Golden
Gate Park (last week in March).

April
Giants games at Candlestick
Park.

SPECIAL EVENTS

San Franciscans enjoy parades

Cherry Blossom Festival,
Japantown (two weekends).
San Francisco Film Festival (late
April–early May).
Opening Day Yachting Season
(late April).

May
Cinco de Mayo Celebration and
parade (4-5 May).
Black and White Ball, Civic
Center.
Armed Forces Day with parade
and festivities at military sites.
San Francisco Examiner Bay to
Breakers Race with up to
100,000 runners.

June
Union Street Spring Festival Arts
and Crafts Fair.
Art Deco Festival, Concourse
Exhibition Center.
Beethoven Festival, Davies Hall
and Herbst Theater.
North Beach Fair, Upper Grant
Avenue.
Stern Grove Midsummer Music
Festival (until August).

Annual Father's Day Kite Festival,
Marina Green.

July
Comedy Celebration Day,
Golden Gate Park.
Jazz and All That Art on Fillmore,
Fillmore Street.
Fourth of July Celebrations and
fireworks in Crissy Field.
International Beer Festival,
Concourse Exhibition Center.
Midsummer Mozart Festival,
Davies Hall and Herbst Theater.
Continuing Midsummer Festival.
Symphony POPS, Civic
Auditorium.

August
Nihonmachi Street Fair,
Japantown.
Football season starts.
Pacific States Crafts Fair, Fort
Mason.
Reggae Explosion, Pier 3, Fort
Mason.
Continuing Mozart Festival,
Symphony POPS, Midsummer
Festival.
Circus time at Cow Palace.

September
San Francisco a la Carte, Golden
Gate Park – annual dining event.
West Coast National Stunt Kite
Championship, Marina Green.
Sausalito Art Festival.
Viewing of the Moon Festival.
San Francisco Fair, Civic Center.
Opera Season begins.
Blues Festival, Fort Mason.
Renaissance Pleasure Faire
(medieval festivities in
Blackpoint Forest).

October
ACT theater season.
Festa Italiana, Pier 45,
Fisherman's Wharf (early part

of the month).
Columbus Day Celebration and parade, North Beach and Fisherman's Wharf.
Grand National Rodeo, Horse Show and Livestock Exposition at Cow Palace.

November

International Auto Show, Moscone Center.
Continuing opera and theater season.

December

Nutcracker ballet, Opera House.
Christmas celebrations.

SPORTS

Participation Sports

Ballooning

Ballooning has become a hot favorite with many visitors but it is expensive and you must be prepared for disappointments if the weather is not right. Flights usually last about an hour and are generally followed by a champagne picnic brunch. The following companies are among those offering this exciting, scenic experience: **Above the West Hot Air Ballooning**, 1019 Vallejo Street (tel: 776-6382), one-hour flights over the Napa Valley with city pick-up available at extra charge; **Balloon Aviation of Napa Valley**, 2299 Third Street, Napa (tel: (707) 252-7067); **Bonaventura Balloon Co**, 133 Wall Road, Napa (tel: (707) 944-2822); **Napa Valley Balloons Inc**, Yountville (tel: (707) 253-2224); **Once in a Lifetime Balloon Co**, Calistoga (tel: (707) 942-6541); **Professor Muldoon's Hot Air**

Balloon Co, Pleasanton (tel: 449-4490).

Bicycling

This is an economic way to get around and San Francisco has two specially signposted scenic cycling routes: one through Golden Gate Park to Lake Merced, the other from the southern end of the city to the Golden Gate Bridge and across to Marin County. There is no shortage of rental bicycle shops with many of them located next to Golden Gate Park, particularly along Stanyan Street and Geary Boulevard. If you like the idea of a personalized four-hour tour that includes equipment and picnic lunch, give **Scenic Cycling Adventours** in Ross a call at 453-0676.

Boating

A popular pastime, boating on the Bay offers incomparable views of the city.
The following companies rent out sailboats and yachts of all sizes.
Ambassador Charters, 1505 Bridgeway, Sausalito (tel: 331-5541); **Blue and Gold Fleet**, Pier 39, Fisherman's Wharf (tel: 781-7877); **Cass' Marina**, 1702 Bridgeway, Sausalito (tel: 332-6789), with sailing school; **D'Anna Yacht Center**, 11 Embarcadero West, Oakland (tel: 451-7000); **Mariner Yacht Charters**, Alameda (tel: 521-0905); **Olympic Circle Sailing Club**, 1 Spinnaker Way, Berkeley (tel: 843-4200), with sailing school; **Spinnaker Sailing Club**, Pier 40, South Beach Harbor (tel: 543-7333).

SPORTS

Gliding

Glider flights are possible all through the year over the Napa Valley at the **Calistoga Soaring Center**, 1546 Lincoln Avenue, Calistoga (tel: (707) 942-5592). Also, over the Bay, from the **Sky Soaring Airport**, 44999 Christy Street, Fremont (tel: 656-9900). Instruction in hang gliding is available at the **Chandelle Hang Gliding Center**, 488 Manor Plaza, Pacifica (tel: 359-6800).

Golf

The city has four public golf courses: the **Golden Gate Park** 9-hole course at 47th Avenue and Fulton Street (tel: 751-8987); Harding Park's 9-hole **Fleming Course** and 18-hole **Harding Park Course**, located at Skyline and Harding Park Boulevard (tel: 664-4690); and **Lincoln Park's** 18-hole course at 34th Avenue and Clement Street (tel: 221-9911).

In the Napa Valley about a 45-minute drive from the city there is a new 27-hole championship course at the **Chardonnay Club**, 2555 Jamieson Canyon Road, Napa Valley (tel: (707) 257-8950). Only 20 minutes from downtown, the **Crystal Springs Golf Club**, 6650 Golf Course Drive, Burlingame (tel: 342-0603) has an 18-hole championship course. One of the toughest courses in northern California is the 18-hole one at **Half Moon Bay Golf Links**, 2000 Fairway Drive, Half Moon Bay (tel: 726-4438), located about 25 miles (40km) south along Highway 1. Fifty miles (80km) north of the city, the **Silverado County Club and Resort**, 1600 Atlas Peak Road, Napa (tel: (707)

257-0200) has two 18-hole courses.

Health Clubs

Many hotels and resorts offer their guests use of health clubs, fitness centers and swimming pools. There is the **Sonoma Mission Inn and Spa**, 18140 Sonoma Highway 12, Boyes Hot Springs, 42 miles/72.5km north of San Francisco, (tel: (707) 938-9000), which features special programs and several luxury properties in the city itself. The Calistoga area (75 miles/120km) north of San Francisco) is a renowned spa area itself where mineral and mud baths and other therapeutic treatments may be taken. Two recommended centers for this are the **Calistoga Spa Hot Springs**, 1006 Washington, Calistoga (tel: (707) 942-6269), and **Dr Wilkinson's Hot Springs**, 1507 Lincoln Avenue, Calistoga (tel: (707) 942-4102).

Horseback riding

Horseback riding is allowed in Golden Gate Park; you can rent horses and take lessons at the **Golden Gate Park Stables** in the park at Kennedy Drive and 36th Avenue (tel: 668-7360) daily except Monday.

River Rafting

River rafting adventures in the vicinity are offered by the **CBOC White Water Rafting Adventures**, Coloma (tel: (916) 621-1236), between March and October. **OARS River Rafting** (tel: (209) 736-4677) operates white-water trips, near Placerville, a two-hour drive from San Francisco; **Outdoor**

Adventures (tel: 663-8300) also organizes white-water trips near the city.

Sportfishing
Among the organizations featuring sportfishing are **Bob Smith's Sportfishing**, 1224 Monticello Road, Lafayette (tel: 283-6773) and **New Easy Rider Sport Fishing**, 561 Prentiss Street (tel: 285-2000). A shop where you can rent fly fishing tackle is **Fly Fishing Outfitters** at 463 Bush Street (tel: 781-3474).

Tennis
There are over 100 public courts scattered throughout the city, 21 in Golden Gate Park alone. There is a nominal charge to use the latter, but the others are all free. One private club which accepts visitors is the **San Francisco Tennis Club** at 645 Fifth Street (tel: 777-9000).

Windsurfing
This activity is at its most popular in Sausalito where **Sausalito Sailboards**, 4000 Bridgeway (tel: 331-9463), offers lessons.

Spectator Sports
Best place to watch **auto racing** is at the **Laguna Seca Raceway**, off Highway 68, between Monterey and Salinas (tel: (408) 373-1811). There are five major annual motor racing events taking place here. Year-round racing takes place at **Sears Point International Raceway**, in the Sonoma Valley off Highways 37 and 121 (tel: (707) 938-8448).

Baseball is best watched in **Candlestick Park**, eight miles (13km) south of the city along the Bayshore Freeway, where the San Francisco Giants play

A breezy day sees windsurfers skimming the waters of the Bay

SPORTS/SPECIAL INTEREST EXCURSIONS

their home games between April and October. There is a downtown box office at 170 Grant Avenue (tel: 982-9400) and an express bus service operates from downtown to the park (call: 673-MUNI for details). Professional **basketball** can be watched at the **Oakland Coliseum Arena** in Oakland (tel: 638-6300) where the Golden State Warriors play between November and April. Direct transportation is available on BART (Bay Area Transit).

For **football** fans the San Francisco 49ers play home games at **Candlestick Park** from August to December; the California Golden Bears play home games in **Memorial Stadium** on the Berkeley University Campus (tel: 642-5150); the University Cardinals play in **Stanford Stadium** on the campus near Palo Alto (tel: 723-1021), from September to November; the Oakland Invaders play home games at the **Oakland Coliseum** from March to June.

Soccer is played by the Golden Bay Earthquakes in the **Spartan Stadium** in San José (tel: (408) 248-4406). The outdoor season runs from May to August. The season for thoroughbred **horse racing** at **Bay Meadows Track** is August to January. The track (tel: 574-7223) is located in San Mateo, off Highway 101, 20 miles (32km) south of the city. From January to June, racing may also be watched at **Golden Gate Fields Track** in Albany on San Francisco Bay, 10 miles (16km) northeast of town off Interstate 10 (tel: 526-3020). The season is from February to June.

SPECIAL INTEREST EXCURSIONS

A favorite way to see the city and its environs is by air, either helicopter or hot air balloon, and a number of operators feature this type of excursion (see **Sports** for ballooning recommendations).

If you would rather keep your feet on the ground or sea, there are again a variety of operators to turn to.

City Tours

Gray Line, 350 Eighth Street, the city's largest tour operator, offers a choice of bus tours in the city and the Bay area. Call 558-9400 for details. If you prefer to go in style, **San Francisco Sightseeing and Tours Inc** (tel: 777-0102) is one of the many operators offering private car (limousine) sightseeing service.

Wine Country

Ami Tours, 808 Post Street (tel: 474-8868) features a half-day "quickie" tour of the Napa Valley that includes a visit to one of the major wineries and tastings at two others.

Carriage Charter, Pier 33, offers a one-hour tour of the Sebastopol vineyards in a horse-drawn carriage daily except Saturday. For special service call (707) 823-7083.

Express Tours (tel: 621-7738) has a full day's program that incorporates tours and tastings at several wineries and allows time for shopping and lunch in historic Sonoma.

Great Pacific Tour Co, 518 Octavia Street (tel: 626-4499) includes lunch and wine tasting in its full day trip to Sonoma and Napa Valley. So does **HMS Tours**, 1057 College Avenue, Santa Rosa (tel: (707) 526-2922), and **Maxi Tours**, 545 Eddy Street (tel: (415) 441-MAXI). **Napa Valley Excursions**, 1825 Lincoln Avenue, Napa (tel: (707) 252-6333), offers a six-hour tour with pick-up in the city by chauffeured car, private winery visits and tours and lunch.

Shopping

If you want to open shop doors that are not always open to the public, maybe **Access to Fashion**, 224 26th Street (tel: 752-5396), is your answer. They will take you hunting for bargains at designer manufacturer outlets in the garment district or for an inside look at some of the city's most stylish boutiques.

Shop 'Til You Drop, 2120 Oaks Drive, Hillsborough (tel: 344-2120), provides shopping professionals who will totally "customize" your shopping trip. **San Francisco Bay Area Shopping Tours**, 690 Market Street (tel: 788-5940), conducts guided shopping tours to eight to ten factory outlets, discount shops and wholesale showrooms.

Walking Tours

City Guides offer free tours of historic Market Street, the Civic Center, North Beach, Victorian Pacific Heights and other parts of the city; call 557-4266 for recorded schedules.

Café Walks, 355 24th Avenue (tel: 751-4286), features historic neighborhood walking tours, scheduled between May and October, otherwise by

There is a good choice of tours of the Napa and Sonoma wine valleys which are well worth a visit

arrangement. The stops at local cafés are always worthwhile.

Chinatown Walking Tours, Pacifica (tel: 355-9657), takes you behind the scenes to back-alley galleries, wholesale markets and a chat with a Chinese cooking teacher. Tours daily at 10:00A.M., sometimes afternoons also.

Helen's Walk Tour, Berkeley (tel: 524-4544), a personalized tour limited to four persons, introduces you to the city on foot and **Chinatown Discovery Tours**, 812 Clay Street (tel: 982-8839), similarly introduces you to Chinatown, two-hour tours departing at 10:00A.M. and 2:00P.M..

Twice a month, the **North Beach Chamber of Commerce** (tel: 673-2522) conducts walking tours of the city's most Bohemian neighborhood.

Nature Tours

A Day in Nature, 1490 Sacramento Street (tel: 673-0548), offers personalized nature tours to Marin Headlands under the guidance of an experienced naturalist.

Friends of Recreation and Parks, McLaren Lodge, Golden Gate Park (tel: 221-1311), features free walking tours of the park with a trained guide. Tours are on weekends from May to October.

Marin Rainbow Tours, San Anselmo (tel: 388-1921), features a trip to the top of Mount Tamalpais, whale watching and a sunset picnic above Lands End, weekends June to November. Muir Woods is one of the most easily reached nature area and several operators offer excursions: **Agentours**, 126 West Portal Avenue (tel: 661-5200), a four-hour narrated daily run tour; and **Cat Tours**, 852 Hensley Avenue, San Bruno (tel: 826-1155), with a 3½-hour trip. Both with Sausalito shopping stop. Farther away, Yosemite National Park beckons. It can be done in a day with **Express Tours** (tel: 243-8195) from May to December, with **Starlane Tours**, 416 Francisco Street (tel: 982-2223) or with **Super Sightseeing Tours**, 123 Townsend Street (tel: 777-5888). See also **Peace and Quiet**, page 64.

Boat Tours

Tours of the harbor operate from Fisherman's Wharf and are a must for all visitors: Forty-five minute daytime cruises depart from Piers 41 or 43½ all year, run by **The Red and White Fleet** (tel: 546-2896), which also operates daily tours to Alcatraz Island. The **Blue and Gold Fleet** (tel: 781-7877) has 1¼-hour harbor trips leaving from Pier 39 at regular intervals.

A boat-trip round the harbor is a "must" for all visitors

DIRECTORY

Contents

Arriving
Camping
Crime
Disabled Travelers
Driving
Emergencies
Entertainment
 Information
Health
Holidays

Liquor Laws
Media
Money Matters
Opening Times
Pharmacist
Places of Worship
Police
Post Office
Public
 Transportation

Senior Citizens
Student and Youth
 Travel
Tax
Telephones
Time
Tipping
Tourist Offices

Arriving

San Francisco's International
Airport is regularly served by a
number of international airlines
including American Airlines,
Delta Airlines, United Airlines
and TWA, all of which have West
Coast representation. It is an
extremely busy airport,
processing more than 1,300
passengers a day. The airport
does have the standard banks,
shops, restaurants, car rental
desks and an information desk
near the baggage claim area.
On the upper level special
phone units in the A T & T
Communications Center allow
callers to pay multilingual
attendants in cash.
Oakland, on the eastern side of
the Bay, and San José on the
southern side of the Bay, also
have their own international
airports.

Transportation into the City

The airport is only 14 miles
(22.5km) from the city, near San
Mateo, and there are a variety of
ways of getting to and from it.

Taxis are available, but fares are
likely to be in excess of $24 flat
rate. There is also limousine
service. Counters from which
this service can be ordered are
located in the baggage claim
areas and fares are up to $60.
San Francisco Super Shuttle (tel:
558-8500) offers a 24-hour mini-
van service to downtown,
Wharf/Lombard,
Sunset/Richmond,
Mission/Castro city districts.
Other companies offering the
service include Lorries (tel: 626-
2113) and Yellow Airport Shuttle
(tel: 282-7433). Pick-up locations
are on the upper level
(departure) at the red-and-white
striped loading zones, fare
approximately $7-$8.
Alternatively, the Door to Door
Airport Express service
operates regularly every 30
minutes from 5:30A.M. to
10:30P.M. for a fare of around $7,
but a reservation for a seat is
necessary (tel: 775-5121). The
journey is about 30 minutes.
Regularly scheduled bus service
between the airport and
downtown (no reservations

necessary) operates every 20 minutes from 5:00A.M. to 11:00P.M.. Look for the Airporter sign at the blue zone on the lower level. Drop-offs are made at some hotels. Fare $7 (Airporter services also operate to Marin County and Sonoma Valley).

Camping
There are campsites within a 30-mile (48km) radius of the city in state parks (advance booking is advisable in the summer). National Park Service information is available at Building 201, Fort Mason Center in San Francisco, CA 94123 (tel: 556-0560).

Crime
Though San Francisco can hardly be described as a safe city, neither is it particularly unsafe – provided you use cautious good common sense and stay away from dark alleys. Parts of the city are a little seedy and San Francisco does have its share of drunks and drug addicts, but act as you would in any major city in the country and things should not go wrong. Areas to avoid are Western Addition and "The Tenderloin." (See **safety**, page 102, for details).

Disabled Travelers
You will find many hotels with some rooms especially designed for those in wheelchairs; there are often disabled toilets and elevator service that features floor numbers in Braille.
For city guide booklets for the disabled in San Francisco call

752-4888 or for public transportation assistance 923-6142 on weekdays or 673-MUNI any time. A recreation center for the handicapped is located at 207 Skyline Boulevard, Lake Merced (tel: 665-4100), with many services free.

Driving
Gas stations and car washes are plentiful. Parking, on the other hand, can be a problem. Main garages can be found at Fisherman's Wharf, 665 Beach Street at Hyde Street (tel: 673-5197 for rates and hours); downtown at 833 Mission Street (tel: 982-8522); at Mason and Ellis Streets (tel: 771-2782); at the Moscone Center, 255 Third Street (tel: 777-2782); in Nob Hill at 1045 California Street (tel: 885-2356); in Chinatown at 733 Kearny Street (tel: 982-6353), and in the Union Street area at 1910 Laguna Street (tel: 563-9820).

Breakdown and Services
American Automobile Association (AAA) members will probably have the easiest time in case of breakdown. In San Francisco the AAA-affiliated drivers' club is the California State Automobile Association, at 150 Van Ness Avenue (tel: 565-2012). Its office is open Monday to Friday 8:30A.M.–5:00P.M.. In the case of a breakdown members can call the office at 565-2012 or try the AAA nationwide emergency road service number, 1-800-336-HELP; callers are given information for obtaining emergency roadside

assistance.

Car Rental
The major car rental companies
with airport service are Alamo
(call (800) 327-9633, Avis (call
(800) 331-1212), Budget (call
(800) 527-0700), Hertz (call
(800) 654-3131) and Thrifty (call
(800) 367-2277). All these
companies have additional city
offices. Other city-based rental
firms include Apple (tel: 348-
0666), Autoexotica (tel: 441-
4779), Bob Leech's Autorental
(tel: 583-2727), Dollar (tel: 673-
2137), Enterprise (tel: 441-3369),
General (tel: 952-4896), National
(tel: 474-5300) and Reliable (tel:
928-4414).

Chauffeured Service
Among the many companies
providing limousine service,
are Chauffeured Limousines
(tel: 344-4400), Executive
Carriage Limousine (tel: 447-
LIMO), Luxury Limousine
Service (tel: 824-6767),
Regency Limousine (tel: 922-
0123), Silver Cloud Limousine
Service (tel: 821-3851), Silver
Star Limousines (tel: 587-0757)
and Triton Limousine Service
(tel: 387-4866).

Parking
Given that San Francisco is
exceptionally hilly and gradients
are steep, the way to park is to
"curb" the tires: turn the tires
toward the street when facing
uphill and towards the curb
when facing down.
This is the law for San Francisco.
Do note the colored zones – the
police department is unlikely to
be kind when it comes to
parking violations.

● The *red* curb zone means no
stopping or parking.
● The *yellow* and *black* limits
commercial vehicles only to half
an hour's loading.
● The *blue* is reserved for the
local disabled.
● The *green* allows a 10-minute
stop.
● The *white* a five-minute stop.
Towaway zones include bus
stops and fire hydrants and fines
can be costly.

Emergencies
In any emergency situation, dial
911 and ask for police, fire
department or ambulance.

Entertainment Information
The daily papers are your best
bet for up-to-date information on
timely events, films and other
entertainment and the Sunday
edition of the *San Francisco
Chronicle* has a *Date Book*,
listing the week's stage, movie
and music entertainment. *Key
This Week in San Francisco* is a
weekly publication with listings
of events, etc. The *San Francisco
and Bay Area Guide* is a free,
weekly publication with an
entertainments section
highlighting special events that
week.
Also look for *Guest Informant*, a
hardcover magazine found in
top hotels.
Information is also available
from the San Francisco Visitor
Information Center, Hallidie
Plaza, Lower Level, Powell and
Market Streets (tel: 391-2000),
open daily 9:00A.M.–5:30P.M.
Monday to Friday, on Saturday
9:00A.M.–3:00P.M. and Sunday
10:00A.M.–2:00P.M.. For a
recorded summary of the day's

events, dial 391-2001/2, a 24-hour service.

Health

If you require a doctor or dentist in a hurry, consult the Yellow Pages or your hotel concierge.

The following organizations are recommended for assistance to travelers:

Access Health Care, 26 California Street (tel: 397-2881): "drop-in" medical care.

American Aeromedical Corp, 655 Skyway Boulevard, San Carlos Airport, San Carlos (tel: 593-1901): around the clock medical and dental assistance that includes hospitalization.

Saint Francis Memorial Hospital, 900 Hyde Street (tel: 775-4321): 24-hour emergency service.

San Francisco Dental Office, 132 The Embarcadero (tel: 777-5115): 24-hour emergency service.

San Francisco General Hospital, 1001 Potrero Avenue (tel: 821-8200): 24-hour emergency service.

Seton Medical Center, 1900

A parking patrolman on duty

Sullivan Avenue, Daly City–call 991-6455 in an emergency.

Holidays

Major holidays which are observed in San Francisco are –
New Year's Day (1 January)
Martin Luther King Jr. Birthday (3rd Monday in January)
Lincoln's Birthday (12 February)
President's Day (3rd Monday in February)
Easter Sunday,
Memorial Day (last Monday in May)
Independence Day (4 July)
Labor Day (1st Monday in September)
Columbus Day (2nd Monday in October)
Thanksgiving Day (usually last Thursday in November)
Christmas Day (25 December).

Liquor Laws

Liquor stores, many groceries and some drug stores all sell alcoholic beverages. Licensing allows for sales between 6:00A.M. and 2:00A.M. and in the case of some hotels/restaurants/nightclubs, later. Most of the latter provide the full range of drinks; in some cases permits only allow the sale of beer and wine.

The legal age for both purchase and consumption of alcohol is 21. Proof of age may well be required.

Media

The main newspapers are the *San Francisco Chronicle* (morning) and *Examiner* (evening), the two combining to produce a Sunday paper. The local communities produce their own paid-for and free publications and papers like the *New York Times* and *USA Today* are readily available. Publications specifically designed for visitors include the *California Calendar*, a monthly listing of entertainment and events throughout northern California; *Guest Informant* (a hardcover magazine you will find in all the top hotel rooms); *Key This Week in San Francisco* (weekly entertainment/events magazine); *Travelhost of San Francisco* (visitor magazine and directory found in hotel rooms). See also **Entertainment Information**, page 119–20. A multitude of national radio stations and television channels operate. Major TV channels are 4(NBC), 5(CBS), 7(ABC) and 9(PBS). Additionally, numerous hotels offer their guests Cable TV and Home Box Office.

Money Matters

The wise visitor will purchase travelers' checks, which can be used much like cash, prior to arrival here. The following all have an exchange facility:
Bank of America, Central Terminal, International Building at the airport (tel: 742-8079), open 7:00A.M.–11:00P.M. daily and at 345 Montgomery Street, Lower Level 1 (tel: 622-2451), open 9:00A.M.–4:00P.M. Monday to Thursday, 9:00A.M.–6:00P.M. Friday and 9:00A.M.–1:00P.M. Saturday.
Heng Loong Foreign Exchange, 626 Jackson Street (tel: 362-8718), open 10:00A.M.–5:30P.M. daily.
Macy's California, Stockton and O'Farrell Streets (tel: 397-3333),

open 9:30A.M.–10:00P.M. Monday to Wednesday, 9:30A.M.–9:00P.M. Thursday and Friday, 9:30A.M.–6:30P.M. Saturday, 11:00A.M.–6:00P.M. Sunday.
Monetary Management of California/Western Union, 201 Third Street (tel: 495-7301), open 8:00A.M.–10:00P.M. Monday to Saturday, 9:00A.M.–6:00P.M. Sunday.
All the major credit cards are widely used and accepted. See also **Tax** and **Tipping**, pages 124 and 125.

Opening Times

Many stores stay open late at least once a week and many are open on a Sunday. Monday is the most frequent closing day for restaurants and museums. However, timings are so variable that you are best off consulting the San Francisco Visitor Information Center, Hallidie Plaza, lower level, Powell and Market Streets (tel: 391-2000). *Their* hours are 9:00A.M.–5:30P.M. Monday to Friday, 9:00A.M.–3:00P.M. Saturday and 10:00A.M.–2:00P.M. Sunday.
Banks are generally open from 9:00A.M. to 4:00P.M. Monday to Friday, though some have longer hours (see also **Money Matters**).
Post Offices Hours are generally 8:00A.M. to 6:00P.M. Monday to Friday and 8:00A.M. to noon on Saturdays.

Pharmacist

Consult the Yellow Pages to locate the nearest pharmacy or ask at your hotel.

Places of Worship

Churches of all denominations

are found in San Francisco. Consult the Yellow Pages or ask at your hotel which appropriate ones are nearby.

Police

If you have a problem that involves the police, you will find Police Department Kobans ("mini-police stations") in Hallidie Plaza (Market and Powell Streets), Chinatown (Grant Avenue) and Japantown (Post and Buchanan Streets) – otherwise in an emergency dial 911.

Post Office

The main post office is at Seventh and Mission Streets. Stamps may be purchased at any post office or, if you have the right change, from machines found in newsagents and gift stores, though expect to pay more with machines.

For opening times of post offices, see page 121.

Public Transportation

A fixed-price fare pays for your ride on either bus or streetcar, including any necessary transfer to any two other vehicles (not including cable cars) within a period of 90 minutes, but you must have exact change. Service on some lines is 24-hour. The three cable car lines run between Powell and Mason, Powell and Hyde, both routes between Union Square and Fisherman's Wharf, while from the foot of Market to Van Ness Avenue runs the California line, between the hours of 6:00A.M. and 1:00A.M.. Maps showing all MUNI routes are available from the tourist information centers.

For schedules, routing details or any other information, call 673-6864.

Cable Cars

MUNI operates the three cable car routes, too. Riders should purchase tickets before boarding – you will see self-service machines at all terminals and major stops. It may well prove economical to purchase the all-day MUNI Pass, valid for all MUNI transportation and available from these machines as well. Three-day MUNI passes are also available from MUNI, the San Francisco Visitor Information Center on Hallidie Plaza and STBS on Union Square. The other advantage of the passes is that they entitle the holder to a discount on admission to many city museums and attractions.

Subway

Everyone seems to appreciate BART (the Bay Area Rapid Transit), the direct subway system that connects the city with the East Bay cities, terminating at Richmond (north), Concord (east), Fremont (south) and Daly City on the West Bay side. BART trains run from 4:00A.M.–midnight Monday to Friday, 6:00A.M.–midnight Saturday and 8:00A.M.–midnight Sunday). An excursion ticket (purchased from dispensing machines) enables you to ride anywhere on the system, but do not go through the computerized exits as this nullifies the ticket. For information dial 788-BART.

Buses

Public transportation is well

organized both within the city and the surrounding counties that spread out across the bridges. Most bus services operate to suburban communities from the Transbay Terminal at First and Mission Streets.

From here **AC Transit** serves the communities in the East Bay area: Berkeley, Oakland, Treasure Island and other cities in Alameda and Contra Costa counties. For information call 839-2882. **Golden Gate Transit** links the city to Marin and Sonoma counties via the Golden Gate Bridge but makes many stops along the route to the bridge. Call 332-6600 for details. **Samtrans** (San Mateo County Transit District) provides a bus service from the city to the Peninsula and serves communities as far south as Palo Alto; there is also a service to San Francisco Airport. Call 761-7000 for information.

Trains

San Francisco is a stop on the national Amtrak rail network; the ticket office is at Transbay Terminal, First and Mission Streets (tel: 872-7245). A daily service operates north to Portland and Seattle and south to Los Angeles and San Diego. Shuttle buses transport passengers between the Transbay Terminal and the main train depot in Oakland. CalTrain operates from the terminal at Fourth and Townsend Streets, a daily rail service south down the peninsula as far as San José. As this is basically a commuter service, there are shuttle buses at peak times from the terminal to the financial district. Call 557-8661 for information.

Ferries

There are two major ferry services: **Golden Gate Ferries** depart from the terminal behind the south wing of the Ferry Building at the foot of Market Street (tel: 332-6600). They offer frequent daily service to Sausalito and to Larkspur in Marin County. There are discounts for children and senior citizens, weekend fares and a special family fare. **Red and White Fleet** are based at Pier 41, Fisherman's Wharf (tel: 546-2896). They operate frequent daily services to Angel Island from Pier 43½, to Sausalito from Pier 43½, to Tiburon from Pier 43½, to Oakland and Alameda from Pier 43½, to Alcatraz Island from Pier 41 and to Marine World/Africa USA/Vallejo several times daily from Pier 41.

Angel Island and Tiburon are also linked by launches across the Raccoon Strait. Call 435-2131 for schedules.

Taxis

Taxis are plentiful though there are the usual problems finding one when it rains. They may be hailed or telephoned for. You could try Luxor Cab (tel: 282-4141) or Veteran's Taxicab Co (tel: 552-1300), and others appear in the Yellow Pages.

Airlines

Among those domestic airlines serving San Francisco are America West (tel: (800) 247-5692)

American Airlines (tel: 398-4434)
Delta Airlines (tel: 552-5700)
USAir (tel: 956-8636)
Southwest Airlines (tel: 885-1221)
TWA (tel: (800) 221-2000)
United Airlines (tel: 428-4322).
Small planes may be chartered for excursions from:
Commodore Helicopters (tel: 332-4482)
Jetstream Aviation (tel: 638-7700)
Kaiserair (tel: 569-9622).

Bus/Coach Services

San Francisco is on the Greyhound/Trailways bus network; the Greyhound depot is at 50 Seventh Street (tel: 558-6789) and the Trailways depot (Transbay Terminal) is at First and Mission Streets (tel: 982-6400). Biggest city bus operator Grayline (tel: 558-9400) has a selection of sightseeing tours within the city. Many tour operators feature packages originating in San Francisco with travel by bus, among them American Express (tel: 362-7954) and California Parlor Car Tours (tel: 474-7500).

Senior Citizens

Some accommodations, restaurants and places to see offer special discounts to senior citizens. Proof of age is necessary to take advantage of these. The following organizations can give information on facilities for the older traveler: American Association of Retired Persons (AARP), 1909 K Street NW, Washington, DC 20049; National Council of Senior Citizens, 925 15th Street NW, Washington, DC 20005. For the Senior

Citizens information line call 626-1033.

Student and Youth Travel

Most places of interest charging an entrance fee do offer a student rate, so it is worth bringing your student ID card.

Tax

The State of California requires an 8.25 percent sales tax on all items except food for preparation and items for out-of-state delivery. This tax may not always appear in the price quoted. San Francisco's hotels and motels do not charge a sales tax but rates are subject to an 11 percent transient tax.

Telephones

Public pay phones are ubiquitous on the street, in terminals, gas stations, restaurants, hotel lobbies and drugstores.
The area code for San Francisco was 415. As of September 1991 the 415 code was split. The new 510 code applies to the East Bay counties of Alameda and Contra Costa (encompassing Oakland, Berkeley, Concord, Pleasanton and Livermore). Unless another area code is given, all phone numbers in this guide are within the 510 area. If in trouble dial 0 for the operator.

Time

California is on Pacific Standard Time which means three hours behind US EST.

Tipping

Since service is not included in a restaurant bill, the average tip is

15 percent of the total bill. Taxi drivers also expect 15 percent and porters expect at least $1 per item.

Tourist Offices

Visitors to San Francisco requiring specific information should write to
San Francisco Convention and Visitors Bureau, 201 3rd Street, Suite 900, San Francisco, California 94103-3185, USA
Tel: (415) 974-6900.
From abroad, contact USTTA (United States Travel and Tourism Administration) in various countries:

UK
22 Sackville Street,
London W1X 2EA
Tel: 071-439 7433

Canada
800 Rochester Boulevard West, Suite 1110, Montreal,

Many visitors arrive in San Francisco by air

Quebec H3B 1X9
Tel: (514) 861-5036
(Plus offices in Toronto and Vancouver)

Australia
Suite 6106, MLC Center, King and Castlereagh Streets, Sydney, New South Wales 2000
Tel: (612) 233-4666

INDEX

ACKNOWLEDGMENTS

The Automobile Association
would like to thank the
following photographers and
libraries for their assistance in
the preparation of this book

BARRIE SMITH took all the
photographs in this book (©AA
Photo Library), including the
cover picture, except:

J ALAN CASH PHOTOLIBRARY
55 Hearst Castle, 57 Santa
Clara,
60 Sonoma.

NATURE PHOTOGRAPHERS
LTD
63 grey phalarope (P R
Sterry),
64 sealion (M Harris), 66
Trillium ovatem (B Burbidge),
70 rattlesnake (S C Blisserot).

SPECTRUM COLOUR LIBRARY
32 dolphin, 69 Yosemite
National Park, 82 winery, 110
parade,
115 Napa Valley.

ZEFA PICTURE LIBRARY UK
LTD
47 Big Sur Coast, 48 Lake
Tahoe,
52 Napa Valley, 97 Broadway.

Barrie Smith thanks TWA and
King George Hotel.